CONVERSATIONS
WITH MY
BROKER

Conversations with my Broker

by Sid

The portrait of a blinking idiot
The Merchant of Venice

HABERFIELD EDITIONS
TUNBRIDGE WELLS

Published in the UK by
Haberfield Editions
Beechhurst
Hurstwood Lane
Tunbridge Wells
Kent

All characters are fictitious

British Library in Publication Data
Sid
  Conversations with my broker.
  I. Title
  823'.914 [F]

  ISBN 0-9515570-0-9

Design and production by Words & Images, Speldhurst, Kent
Set in Plantin by Vitaset, Paddock Wood, Kent
Printed and bound by Biddles Ltd, Guildford, Surrey

This strange disease of modern life
Matthew Arnold

1. Ledger domain

Okay, I'll come straight out with it. I was a bit pickled by the time I left the Dorchester (or was it Claridge's? I can't remember). Soused in champagne and all on the house. I wasn't even asked to chip in for the pate de foie. Did you know that Gandhi – the real one, not Ben Whatsisname – kept a goat at Claridge's? Liked fresh meat for his curry, I believe. But I digress. What would a fellow like me be doing at Claridge's, swilling champagne with the stars of stage, screen and Page Three? (It was the Dorchester, now I come to think of it. So much for Gandhi's goat.)

Well, need you ask? Unless I had joined the catering staff, which I hadn't, or popped in for a leak, there could be only one explanation: young Sid had come into money. Loads and loads of beautiful money. In other words, I had won the pools. How else could a working-class lad make the grade in our enterprise culture? Not much enterprise down Fulham way – or culture, for that matter. So that explains it, doesn't it? Here was I, at the Dorchester, getting my cheque from this bird with the enormous boobs (or enlarged mammary glands, as Gandhi would have said). It was a bit of a struggle to keep my hands off the goods, I can tell you. But I didn't like the look of this bloke with the camera. Had a proprietorial air about him. Lay one finger on her and I'd be all over Page Three myself. As an obituary. Anyway, the cheque was more important. Would it change my life, some idiot from the gutter Press wanted to know. Well, if it didn't, not much point in winning, eh? I sometimes wonder where reporters dream up their questions. But I'm getting ahead of myself. Let me explain.

I haven't always been rich. No Rothschild or Kennedy blood in my veins, worse luck. For most of my life, I've been at the mercy of the bank manager. A succession of bank managers, in fact. For some reason, they all seemed to think I'd be better off elsewhere. The one that was supposed to listen actually suggested that I opened an account at the Post Office.

'Try Girobank,' he said. 'They don't have to make a profit. We do.'

Terse and to the point, I thought. But I didn't take his advice. I read somewhere that there are six hundred different banks in the United Kingdom. I figured that even if I went through one a month that little collection should last me fifty years. By the time I had worked through the list, the guy in charge of overdrafts at the first one would be dead and I could start all over again.

I don't understand the mentality of some bank managers. You'd think it was their money they were trying to protect. I've always taken the view that banks were there to lend money. I mean, what's the point of leaving all that dough in the vault to gather dust when it could be helping young, thrusting entrepreneurs like me to pay the rent? Doesn't make sense.

My mate Frankie, a Geordie who had come south to get a job and ease the burden on the welfare state, was in the same boat as me: skint. But, for a Geordie, Frank was pretty clued up when it came to juggling with figures.

'Listen,' he said. 'We've both got current accounts, haven't we?'

'Ye...s,' I said, not wishing to argue over technicalities.

'Then why don't we give each other a million quid?'

'Because I haven't got a million quid, that's why.'

'No, but the bank has.'

The penny dropped. In fact, several pennies dropped and promised to roll in my direction.

'Just a bookkeeping entry,' explained Frank. 'You write out a cheque for me and I'll do the same for you. It'll do wonders for our credit ratings. Next time you want a loan, they'll bust a gut to empty the piggy bank.'

Well, it seemed like a good idea at the time. I could just imagine that pin-striped creep with the rimless specs. falling over himself when he saw that I had come into money. I could just picture him rushing across the street with a million smackers in his executive briefcase and dumping them on the counter at Frank's bank. At the same time (or, preferably, a couple of minutes earlier), Frank's bloke would be heading my way with a plastic bag full of the means of exchange. I thought I might report sick and go down and watch the fun. Instead, I got a phone call from the creep with the rimless specs.

'Mr Arbuthnot?' he enquired.

'That's me,' I replied, not without a touch of pride.

'Mr Arbuthnot,' he said. 'I have here a cheque, drawn by you, for one million pounds. Did you wish the bank to honour this cheque?'

'Of course. I wouldn't have written it otherwise.'

'Then perhaps you would be kind enough to forward sufficient funds?'

Jesus! I thought. Something must have gone wrong. If he had my cheque, where was Frank's? Don't say the computer had gobbled it up, in the same way that it had chewed up my plastic meal ticket one day.

'I think you'll find,' I said, hoping that Little Miss Big Ears at the next desk was actually doing some work for once, 'that the money will arrive shortly.'

'If you're referring to the cheque for one million pounds, drawn in your favour by Mr Brannigan, then, yes, that has arrived. But I understand that Mr Brannigan is in the same impecunious position as yourself.'

Well, how's that for banking confidentiality? How did he know that Frank was in Queer Street unless he had been discussing our private financial affairs with his mate across the street? A case for the Ombudsman, I reckon.

'I don't understand . . . ' I began.

'Oh, I think you do, Mr Arbuthnot. And let me tell you that I am not very amused. If you were not already in debt to the bank I should tell you to take your account elsewhere. Now, do you want me to pay this one million pounds, which I can let you have at an overnight rate of fifteen per cent?'

'Don't bother,' I said. 'I can probably get by without it.'

Sadist! Couldn't even see the funny side of our little joke. But that's bankers for you. No imagination. I expect they get a kick out of quoting the rules, especially to widows and orphans and others too poor to argue. Just wait till one of them appears in the dock at the Old Bailey, accused of fiddling the books. I'll be in the public gallery, waiting to put the boot in.

I met Frank at the Cock and Feathers for a quick couple of halves after work.

'I think I might emigrate to Australia,' said Frank. 'From what I hear, you can live pretty cheap in the bush on walrus and platypus tails.'

'Don't you mean wallaby?' I asked, recalling some furry things I had seen at the zoo.

'Yeah, well,' growled Frank, downing the first half as though already in training for the six o'clock swill, 'maybe I'll settle for shark's fin soup.'

As it turned out, I had got off pretty lightly. Frank's mob had told him to close the account there and then. In fact, they handed him a cheque for the balance, less charges, which, the manager pointed out, did not include interest on one million pounds.

'I thought they would have been impressed,' said Frank. 'After all, not everybody has a million quid.'

True, I had to admit.

When I got home, there were a couple of letters waiting for me. Mrs Szaranski, the landlady, gave them to me herself. She didn't say anything but I could tell by the look in her eye that she was wondering when I was going to pay the two weeks rent that were owing.

'Thanks, Mrs S.,' I said, taking the envelopes and hurrying to my room.

One was from the credit card company. Did I know that my limit had been exceeded? (Well, yes, I did know. I was hoping they wouldn't mention it, though.) In fact, they seemed quite relaxed about it. 'If your present limit is insufficient, please let us know,' they said. I would, immediately. The thing that gets up my nose is that most of these card companies are owned by the banks. That's why the cunning devils in the High Street won't lend you any money. They know that, if you're desperate for a quid or two, you'll be forced to borrow from their little plastic offshoot. At twice the rate of interest. Daylight robbery, I call it. In the old days, you'd be in the nick if you tried to charge that much for money. Now they just say it's due to market forces.

The other letter was from the pools company in Liverpool. I hadn't done the pools for a month or two, mainly because the last time I wrote out a cheque for the treble chance the manager bounced it.

'We do not finance gambling,' he said.

Not finance gambling? I ask you! Where does he think all that money to buy stocks and shares on the Stock Exchange comes from? Not from Frank and me. I was reading somewhere – in that book about the Great Crash by that American chap, I think it was – that half the money that propped up the stock market during the 1920's came from the banks. Anyway, I didn't argue. When I checked the coupon I hadn't won so he had done me a favour. Mind you, he didn't do my credit rating much good in Liverpool. But maybe they don't worry about that sort of thing up there. The poor understand what it's like to be poor.

Well, Sid, what about it? You've got to be in it to win it, as they say in Australia. Trouble was, as you know as well as I do, there was a slight problem over funds. I was playing football, not cricket, and one bouncer was enough. Should I tap Mrs S. for a fiver? No, that was too risky. She might demand the rent there and then, and chuck me out if it were not forthcoming. But when you're desperate, desperate measures are needed. What did those SAS blokes say before they knocked hell out of the Ayatollah's embassy? Who dares wins? Dare I write out a cheque? What was there to lose? Nobody was going to worry about a small thing like the stake money if I won. I sat down and filled in the coupon.

Just to add a little spice to the proceedings (a frisson, as the Frogs say), I used all the numbers from the top of my cheque book – sorting code, account number, etc. I could have used the numbers provided by the Daily Smut but I reckon if they knew who was going to win they wouldn't be writing for the newspapers. They'd be sitting on the beach at Costa del Crumpet, admiring the view. So, I wrote out a cheque for five pounds and 22 pence, shoved it in the envelope and walked down to the corner to post it. I just hoped that some poor bugger in Liverpool, as skint as I was, wouldn't do a bunk with the cheque.

Well, you can guess what happened. Saturday afternoon, as soon as the wrestling was out of the way, I checked the results on the telly. Would you believe it? Twenty four points! Thank God for the SAS! Of course, it might be one of those weeks when everybody had twenty four points and they cancelled half the dividends. But, no, the little geezer with the grey hair said 'possible jackpot'. It's just as well I don't suffer from high blood pressure. I rushed downstairs and burst in on Mrs S. just as she was about to have a little nip of something from the bottle.

'I've done it!' I cried, grabbing the bottle and taking a swig for myself. 'I've cracked it!'

'Cracked what?' asked Mrs S., eyeing me coldly.

'The pools! I've won the pools! I'm rich! I'm rich!'

'In that case,' said Mrs S., her eyes warming ever so slightly, 'you'll be able to pay the rent.'

'You shall have it, my love, and more – just as soon as I get the cheque.'

I don't know what made me call her 'my love'. I can't stand the old boot. But the words seemed to have a miraculous effect.

'Let me get a glass,' she said, 'and we'll have a noggin to celebrate.'

'If you don't mind, I'll just use your phone to make sure I've won.'

'Help yourself,' she said, pouring a large measure of best British sherry. 'How much do you think you've won?'

'I've no idea,' I said. 'Could be the jackpot.'

'Oh, my God!' cried Mrs S. 'And we've got no champagne.'

I don't know what Mrs S. was thinking as she listened to the phone call. All I know is that the girl on the other end confirmed that I had a winning entry.

'We'll be in touch as soon as we've worked out the dividend,' she said.

I didn't like to ask about the cheque.

'Bottoms up!' said Mrs S., raising her glass.

'Cheers!' I replied. 'I'll buy you a whole barrel of this stuff when I can get my hands on the loot.'

'Oh, you are a caution, Mr Arbuthnot! Is there anything I can do for you?'

Well, I don't mind telling you that the world was beginning to look a very different place that Saturday afternoon. No longer was Mrs S.'s front door a place to sidle past as quickly as possible, praying that she would not appear and demand the rent. Even the net curtains and the chintzy furniture had a certain charm about them. And now I came to look at her closely, Mrs S. had a touch of quality about her, too. A bit worn, perhaps, but a fine-looking woman. I wondered if she'd be offended if I offered to buy her a face-lift.

Unfortunately, in my haste to send off the coupon I had omitted to put an X in the little box to say that I didn't want any publicity. Before I could even think of what charity to support, they had arranged for me to go to the Ritz to collect a cheque for – wait for it! – nine hundred and sixty eight thousand, four hundred and fourteen pounds. Not quite a million, but, with the help of Ernie at the Premium Bond office, it wouldn't take long to reach the magic figure.

The thought made me go quite weak at the knees. Me, Sid, a millionaire! Blimey! What would me old Mum – God rest her soul – have said? Or the old man, for that matter? Neither of them knew the first thing about finance. Always put their trust in their elders and betters, especially when the Tories were in power. I guess that's why I grew up to be an economic illiterate. I mean, if you've been brought up, like the Rothschilds, with a silver spoon in your mouth, you know when somebody is trying to palm you off with aluminium. It's not until you get a couple of spoons yourself that you can tell the difference. Mrs S. was so overcome by the thought of getting the rent on time that she quoted me a line or two from some poem.

> How pleasant it is to have money, heigh-ho,
> How pleasant it is to have money.

I'll say 'Cheers!' to that!

Of course, the danger of giving lots of dough to a bloke like me is that he'll squander it on booze and birds and holidays in the Bahamas, that sort of thing. What would Sid Arbuthnot know about money? Nothing. He has never kept any long enough to get on familiar terms with it. In one pocket and out the other. I must say the people from the pools company were pretty good. They offered to put me in touch with all sorts of experts who could advise me on investments. Gold, gilts (I always thought they were pigs), unit trusts, property. You name it, they mentioned it. But what I say is, never mind the interest, just feel the boodle. To invest for 'long-term growth' is a bit like telling one of them poor devils rescued from Belsen 'Hang on till next week and you can have a slap-up Kosher nosh'. What he wants is a bloody great steak right now. Same with money. You can take the advice later so long as you've got the cash now. To feel rich, you've got to have a few quid in your pocket; you know, so as you can go into the Savoy and say, 'Deux escargots on toast, please, James, and be quick about it'. I might even buy Frank a first-class ticket to Australia, if that's what he wants. After all, he's my mate and you can't drop him just because you've suddenly got a few quid. I mean, suppose the boot was on the other foot and Frank had won a million? I'd feel pretty cut up if he didn't chuck a few quid my way. All this investment stuff can come later, when you've got over the shock.

Being rich, I soon discovered, has its drawbacks. First of all, there was the problem of the cheque. (Well, actually, that's not quite right. The first problem was the champers. Goes to your head if you're not used to it.) But the cheque was a problem, nevertheless. Nine hundred and sixty eight thousand quid is not to be sneezed at. I couldn't walk round London with all that loot in my pocket, especially now that I'd posed for the papers with the bird with the big tits. I might be mugged, or worse. To be quite honest, I didn't fancy paying it in to the bank, the very same bank that less than a week ago had given me a little lecture on the ethics and etiquette of banking. Still, what could I do? If you can't beat 'em, join 'em. So, as soon as I could shake off all the freeloaders and hangers-on (PR men, I think they were called), I slipped out the side door and walked up Oxford Street looking for a bank.

I don't know what they put in the champers at the

Dorchester but it has a kick like Gandhi's goat. I must have walked past dozens of banks because the first one I noticed happened to be a branch of the Bank of Kuwait. Very posh, these Arab banks, you know. Not like some banks I could mention, where you've got to stand in a queue a mile long while the security camera gives you the once-over for a possible Identikit. You could see they were used to handling a lot of money because the wog – sorry, teller – behind the counter didn't bat an eyelid when he took the cheque and the giro slip. He just stamped it, gave me a receipt and popped the cheque in a drawer with hundreds of others. Bit of an anti-climax, really. All that shemozzle at the Dorchester – birds, booze and ballyhoo – and this little Arab couldn't care less. That's life, I suppose. When you've seen one, you've seen them all, as the sinner said to the salvationist. Next week, there'll be another winner and I'll be just part of history.

To tell the truth, I'd had more than a skinful of champers. Made a bit of a pig of myself, seeing as how it was on the house. The old head was going round and round as I walked up Oxford Street (I think it was Oxford Street) and the traffic whizzing around Marble Arch didn't help. I felt like throwing up. What a way to end the most marvellous day of my life! Get yourself out of the public view, Sid, before you make a real fool of yourself, I said.

I hailed a taxi.

'Fulham Broadway,' I said, 'and careful how you take the corners.'

'You all right, mate?' the driver said. 'I don't want you throwing up in my cab. You'll clean it up, if you do.'

'I'll have you know, my man,' I said, 'that I've just won the pools.'

'In that case, I'll expect a bloody good tip.'

Surly lot, London cabbies. They had to take what they got when I was poor.

Would you believe it, when we arrived I hadn't got a cent to pay the fare? All that money in the bank and not a penny in the pocket. The driver was about to turn nasty when, bless her heart, Mrs S. tottered down the front steps with her purse in her hand. She was, I had discovered over the previous few days, an extremely generous lady, simply misunderstood. She gave the cabbie a right earful and saw me to my bed. That's all I remember until about half past ten the following morning. Crickey! What a hangover! Mrs S. was very good, though. She put a bag of ice on my head and made me some strong, black coffee. I could feel the caffeine rushing about, stimulating whatever it was supposed to stimulate.

'You just take it easy, Mr Arbuthnot,' she said. 'There's no need to get up. You just lay there until you're feeling like it.'

I didn't feel like it, or anything else. But there was no reason why I, Sid Arbuthnot, should remain in bed this fine summer's morning when I had a million quid in the bank and lots of new friends. Except, that is, for a blinding headache. Still, Mrs S. had dissolved some aspirin in a glass that had a hint of the hair of the dog about it but I swallowed it, nevertheless. In about half an hour, I felt much better and got up.

'Special delivery,' said Mrs S., waving an envelope at me when I came down for breakfast. 'I suppose you'll be getting a lot of these now?'

Begging letters by express delivery, I thought. Well, they can't be that hard up if they can afford Royal Mail Datapost.

I stared at the words on the front of the envelope. The sun seemed very bright this morning.

'From the bank,' said Mrs S., with a knowing look. 'I expect you're a VIP customer now.'

How did she know, the old haybag? Been reading my mail while I was out for the count. Steaming open the envelopes, then sealing them up again in the hope I wouldn't notice. No, Sid, I told myself, that was unworthy of you. Now you are rich, you must banish these uncharitable thoughts. Mrs S. has proved herself to be a woman with a heart of gold.

'Aren't you going to open it?' she enquired.

'All in good time,' I said.

Old habits die hard, especially when you're dealing with the bank. Caution was the watchword. I took a knife and slit the envelope gently open. Mrs S. was right: it was from the bank. The manager had probably seen my picture in the Daily Smut. I expect he wanted to apologise. A little grovel to keep on the right side of me.

Dear Sir (he wrote),

I had hoped that, following our conversation of last week, you would refrain from further abuse of the banking system.

Despite my hopes, I have this morning received a giro credit from the Bank of Kuwait for £968,414. I have no doubt that the Bank of Kuwait will take the appropriate measures in due course.

In the meantime, I insist that you close your account immediately.

Yours faithfully,
B.F. Collier
Customer Liaison

Well, by the time I had read it six times the message began to sink in. Mrs S. thought it was hilarious. So did I, now that I saw what he was trying to get at. So, the pin-striped git who had made my life difficult during the three months or so that I had favoured him with my custom had dropped an almighty clanger. Not only that but he had spent a couple of quid trying to impress me with his efficiency.

'Right,' I said, buttering the toast that Mrs S. had placed in front of me. 'As soon as I've eaten, we'll go down and close the account. You had better bring your big shopping bag, Mrs S.'

Straight after breakfast, we walked up the High Street to oblige the manager. Mrs S. was looking quite chirpy in the sunshine. A fine-looking woman in her prime, she must have been. Pity she had let herself go. We reached the bank and went inside.

'You wait here with the bag,' I said, 'while I sort this bugger out.'

I pressed the bell at the end of the counter. Securities, foreign currency and enquiries, said a notice over the grille. Nobody seemed in much of a hurry. I pressed again.

I had a strong feeling that people were looking at me. I glanced up at the ceiling. The little camera there had its evil eye poking right in my direction. I could see myself in the lens. Bit scruffy, I thought. More like Sir Bob Geldorf on safari than a guy with a million quid in the bank. Perhaps it was because I hadn't shaved and the old eyes were a bit bloodshot, courtesy of Claridge's (or was it The Ritz?). Eventually, a bloke appeared on the other side of the grille. To say that he was friendly would be stretching a point. Suspicious, yes; friendly, no.

'Yes?' he enquired, squinting through his miserable bifocals.

'I've come to close my account.'

'You have an account here?'

'I wouldn't have come here at this time of day to close it unless I had, would I?' I shot back.

'I don't know why you would come here at any time of the day, sir,' he replied, casting a nervous glance at Mrs S., who was rummaging in her bag.

'Well, I wouldn't. So pull your finger out and hand over the money.'

At that, a very strange thing happened. The grille through which we had been conversing so pleasantly snapped shut and all hell broke loose. Uriah Heep did the fastest vanishing trick I've ever seen and the tellers all disappeared from view. The camera made an incredible whirring sound and, somewhere offstage, a bell began to ring.

'Just our luck to arrive in the middle of a fire drill,' I remarked, joining Mrs S. at the little table where she had made herself at home.

'They probably think you've come to rob the bank,' she said, faintly amused.

'They could be right,' I said. 'Robbery with a few menaces, if they don't get a move on.'

After about thirty seconds, the bell stopped ringing and the fire drill came to an end. A little guy with a white moustache and very bright eyes poked his head nervously around the door.

'Can I help you, sir?' he enquired.

'If it's not too much trouble, I'd like to close my account,' I said, wondering how many more times I would have to tell them.

'Your name, sir?'

'Arbuthnot. Sid Arbuthnot.'

'Ah! Mr Arbuthnot.'

I don't know if you've ever heard the air rushing out of a tyre that has just been punctured but that's what the little guy sounded like. He looked just as flat.

'Why didn't you say?' he asked, emerging from the doorway.

'Nobody asked me. Now, if you wouldn't mind handing over the money, I'd be much obliged.'

'Certainly, sir,' he said, perking up and signalling to somebody in the distance. 'I'll close the account with pleasure but I don't think there'll be much of a balance.'

'Just short of a million quid, I think.'

'And you'd like it all in cash, I suppose?' he said, sarcastically.

'Yes, please.'

'If you'd care to wait a moment, Mr Arbuthnot, I'll see what I can do.'

'Thank you so much.'

'I don't think he believes you,' said Mrs S., with what my old mum would have called deep psychological insight.

'He'll learn.'

By this time, the tellers had returned to their cages and were glancing at us surreptitiously, trying to pretend that nothing had happened. I think the RSPCA should be brought in to look at these cages, you know. Not enough room in some of them to swing a cat.

Mr Bright Eyes waltzed up, clutching a slip of paper and a handful of loose change.

'Here we are, sir,' he said. 'Your closing balance, including interest and charges, three pounds and forty eight pence.' He indicated the slip of paper. 'If you would just sign here.'

'What about the rest?' I asked.

'The rest, sir?'

'Yes. The nine hundred and sixty eight thousand quid that arrived from the Bank of Kuwait.'

'Oh, that? We paid the milkman with it.'

'In that case, you had better start drinking your tea black, chum, because I am not leaving here without it.'

'Please yourself, Mr Arbuthnot. But I should point out that

we close at half past three, at which time the doors are locked. Unless you wish to sleep on the floor, I suggest you leave before then. Now, I'm a very busy man and I must bid you goodday.'

He turned to go but as he was only a little half-pint I grabbed him by the lapel.

'Listen, buddy,' I said, 'either I get that money or you personally will feel the ire of a wealthy man.'

I rather liked that phrase. I was going to say 'or you personally will get a punch on the nose'. But a wealthy man can control his temper more easily than a poor one. Just as well, because at that moment the cops rushed in.

I don't know if it was because I still had my hand on the creep's lapel or because my Gillette had not been functioning too well. But before I could say 'Good morning, officers' I was on the ground, staring at a Size Eleven boot. I could feel another one resting gently on my neck. They say there's no police brutality in Britain. I, Sid Arbuthnot, would like to say otherwise. A Size Eleven boot with a fifteen-stone copper in it is what the beak might call prima facist evidence.

Somewhere above, I could hear Mrs S. screaming abuse. For a foreigner, she knew some right British phrases. Suddenly, the copper winced and the pressure on my neck eased. A fine woman, Mrs S., with a useful knowledge of anatomy. I stood up.

The creep with the three pound forty eight was having an animated conversation with the creep with the rimless specs. The chief copper was waving his truncheon and trying to stop people escaping from the bank. The copper who had left his footprint on my best shirt was lying on the ground, groaning. Mrs S. stood over him, looking very pleased with herself. The manager, who at last had emerged from his inner sanctum, appeared to be on the verge of a nervous breakdown. His left eye twitched uncontrollably. The tellers counted their money and pretended not to notice.

'I think,' said the manager, when the injured constable had been removed from the scene, 'that there has been a terrible mistake.'

'Oh, really?' I said. 'I thought this was perhaps how you

treated everybody who came to close an account.'

The manager withdrew a small silk handkerchief from his breast pocket and wiped his brow. The man was obviously a complete wreck.

'I'm afraid we owe you the most frightful apology, Mr Arbuthnot,' he began, trying to control his nervous tic.

'That's not all you owe me,' I said. 'There's a small matter of a million quid.'

'Quite. But if you would care to step into my office, I'm sure we can discuss the matter amicably.'

'Nothing doing,' I said. 'I've come to collect a million quid and I'm not leaving here without it. So, if you would open your safe, my good fellow, I'll be getting along. I have my investment strategy to consider.'

'Oh, well, if it's investment advice you're after, we have a whole team of advisers just waiting to help valued customers like yourself, Mr Arbuthnot.'

'Ex-customer,' I reminded him.

'Very well, Mr Arbuthnot. But may I say how sorry I am to lose your account?'

'You may. Now run along, my good man, and don't keep me waiting. Time is money, you know.'

I could see that Mrs S. approved of my attitude. The cops had taken her name and said they would be in touch. But at least they hadn't arrested her – and she still had her shopping bag. I smiled encouragingly at her as the manager and the creep with the rimless specs. ran up and down the cages, grabbing handfuls of dough. Eventually, the pathetic slaves of capitalism were forced to admit defeat.

'I'm sorry, Mr Arbuthnot,' said the slave with the nervous tic, 'but we don't appear to have that much money in the bank at the moment. Would you care to take a cheque?'

'I've already had one cheque which I paid into the Bank of Kuwait,' I told him. 'And so far I haven't seen a penny of it. I want cash, here and now.'

'Well, you can't have it,' the manager replied, trying desperately to save face in front of his staff.

'Can't have it?' I repeated, in my friendly, Ronnie Biggs

fashion.

'We don't keep that amount of cash at the bank. This is only a small branch and not all of our very valued customers win the football pools.'

'Lucky for you – or you wouldn't have many customers left by now.'

The girls in the cages were beginning to titter. Uriah Heep looked as if he was about to have a heart attack. Either that or they had locked the loo during the fire drill.

'How much can you let me have now?' I demanded.

'We could let you have, maybe, half a million,' the manager replied airily.

'All right. I'll take that and you can deliver the rest to my residence later.'

'You are being very dificult,' the manager sighed. 'If you take half a million, you will leave us with nothing in the till.'

'You should have thought of that before writing nasty letters,' I replied.

The long and the short of it is that, after about half an hour, Mrs S. and I were invited into the office to take possession of a huge pile of money. There it was, spread all over the manager's desk.

'I assume that you will not wish to be burdened down with coin?' the manager said, a trifle sarcastically, I thought.

'No, but I'll have three pounds forty eight, if you don't mind – just in case it gets overlooked in the rush.'

Well, you could have cut the air with a knife as we counted through all the money in the wreck's little empire. But why should I feel guilty, I thought? It's mine; I'm entitled to it. So tough luck if the milkman has to rely on the petty cash.

The subject of the upcoming RSPCA investigation put down the telephone and turned to me.

'Securicor will deliver the rest after lunch,' he announced.

By now, it was well after two o'clock, anyway. I could see why the banks want to do away with notes and plug us in to silicon chips; counting the loot can be a time-consuming business. Not only for Mrs S. and me but for the couple of flunkies detailed to keep an eye on us. They missed their lunch break. There was a fiver short in one bundle but, by now, I couldn't be bothered.

'Okay,' I said. 'Have the rest at my place by four o'clock or I'll have to charge interest.'

'We'll do our best,' the manager promised, sounding like a wolf cub at a girl guide orgy, 'but, of course, it's out of our hands now.'

'You can say that again, old cock,' I said, tossing a bundle of fivers to Mrs S., who stuffed them in her bag.

The wreck twitched violently but refrained from further comment. One heart attack was enough for one day.

As we walked home, I reflected on the little poem that Mrs S. had quoted earlier. How pleasant it was to have money.

Heigh-ho!

2. Real disposable income

Friday, July 13. Spent morning in court, trying to get Mrs S. off a charge of assaulting the police. Hired expensive lawyer in striped pants. Amazing what money can buy. Our man tied opposition in knots. Fuzz lucky not to be charged with causing an affray. Case dismissed, with costs. Took Mrs S. out to lunch.

I don't know if you've ever tried to book a table in London but unless you've got contacts you might as well take sandwiches to the park. Some of these snooty sods who mark up plonk for a living ought to remember who keeps them in business. Customers, like me.

'Mr Arbuthnot?'

Pregnant pause, like what you get when they're checking your credit card.

'I'm awfully sorry, sir, but we're booked solid for the next seven days.'

Lying hound. I bet if he'd seen my picture in the Daily Smut he'd have found us a seat, all right. And a double helping of salmonella. Mrs S. wanted to go to the greasy-spoon dago joint around the corner so that we wouldn't be away from home for very long. She was worried about all that money under the mattress. Suppose the house burned down, she said? Fat lot of good a million quid's worth of charred banknotes would be.

'Stop worrying, or you'll get indigestion,' I told her. 'We're going to have a decent meal and that's that. I know, we'll go to the Savoy.'

'Are you sure they'll let us in?' asked Mrs S.

'There'll be trouble if they don't,' I replied. 'My money's as good as anybody else's.'

But I could see that Mrs S. was not happy with the situation. Bit out of her depth, I think. The fact that we were nearly run over by a taxi going the wrong way up that little side street didn't help. In the end, we found ourselves at one of those Italian joints off Covent Garden: you know, all spaghetti and garlic. The waiter smelled our money the moment we walked through the door.

'Might I suggest a bottle of champagne, sir?' he ventured, flashing the wine list in front of me. 'It goes well with the lobster.'

'No champers for me,' I said. 'I'm still getting over the last lot. But you can bring us half a carafe of the house red.'

His face fell half a mile. Cheeky devil, I thought. That'll teach him to treat customers by the size of their wallet. Besides, pouring champagne down the throat of Mrs S. was like feeding strawberries to donkeys. She wouldn't have appreciated it. In any case, she was anxious to get home.

'Stop worrying,' I said. 'The front door's locked and bolted and nobody knows where the money is. It'll be perfectly safe. Now, relax and enjoy your meal.'

The bill came to £8.64. I gave the waiter a tenner.

'Keep the change,' I said.

We took a taxi all the way to Fulham. This was becoming a bit of a habit, I thought. I didn't want the neighbours to think that I was flaunting my wealth. I'd already had 154 begging letters – some of them from quite good addresses – and there was no point in provoking more. As we turned the corner by the Hospital for Nervous Diseases, I told the driver to stop. We'd walk the last few yards.

'You've got to do something about all this money,' said Mrs S., looking very flustered as we entered her bedroom. 'You can't leave it here. It's not safe.'

'Why? Nobody's going to be sleeping in your bed, except you, are they? And you're not going to run off with it.'

Mrs S. shot me a very old-fashioned look. But I had to admit she had a point. In fact, she had put her finger on a problem faced by all us millionaires sooner or later: the problem of wealth. It's all very well having money but you've got to look after it. All these stories about how wonderful it is to be rich simply ignore the other side of the coin. Instead of worrying about whether you can afford to eat at the end of the week you worry in case somebody breaks in and runs off with your fortune. Suppose the house burns down, as Mrs S. had already intimated? Suppose a special sort of termite found only in boarding-house mattresses gobbles it all up in the night? You'd look a right Charlie taking a handful of bacterial remains to the Bank of England and saying, 'There's a million quid here, mate. Could you give us some new notes?' I bet nobody's tried that one before, though.

'Well, what shall we do with it?' I asked.

'Take it back to the bank,' advised Mrs S. promptly.

'You must be joking! I'm not letting that bunch of rogues get their hands on it again.'

'You've got to be sensible about this,' said Mrs S., sounding like a Dutch uncle. 'Just because they've given you a hard time in the past, it doesn't mean they'll bounce your cheques now you've come into money.'

'They won't if they know what's good for them,' I muttered, wondering how the old haybag knew that several pages of my paying-out book had been returned, marked 'Refer to drawer'.

'Take my advice,' Mrs S. continued. 'Now you're a millionaire, put aside a few quid for a rainy day. Make your money start working for you. It's doing no good here. Might as well keep a white elephant in the garage.'

Until then, I hadn't realised that Mrs S. was a pretty shrewd old bird when it came to money. I suppose that keeping a boarding house must teach you a thing or two. But the thought of handing all that lolly back to that creep of a manager – he was actually in court this morning, giving evidence! – made my blood boil. No way was he going to benefit from my good housekeeping.

'You don't have to take it back to the same bank,' said Mrs S., revealing some familiarity with the system. 'You can open half a dozen accounts, if you like, at different banks.'

Now, that really did appeal to my spirit of adventure.

'Yeah!' I said. 'I could open nine accounts, each with a hundred thousand quid in it!'

'What about the odd sixty eight thousand?' asked Mrs S.

'You could keep that to buy the groceries,' I said. 'On a sort of advanced rent basis.'

A shadow, no bigger than a direct debit, passed swiftly over Mrs S.'s face. Her eyes clouded and her upper lip quivered slightly. I thought the plonk was about to claim a victim. But, no. Mrs S. had weightier matters on her mind.

'I've been meaning to get around to this all week,' she croaked.

'Get around to what?' I asked.

'Well, now that you're rich, you can afford to buy a place of your own. You won't want to stay here much longer, will you?'

I laughed.

'Is that all that's bothering you?' I said. 'Well, don't you worry, Mrs S. When I want to leave, I'll give you a month's notice and pay you in full. But, at the moment, I don't plan to go anywhere.'

'Oh, Sid!' she cried, throwing her arms around my neck. 'I'm so glad.'

I could see that the old boot was in danger of becoming sentimental so I changed the subject molto pronto.

'Bring me the Yellow Pages,' I said, 'and let's see if we can find a bank I haven't been chucked out of in the past.'

'What you need is the Bankers' Almanac,' said Mrs S. 'That'll give you a much better selection than the Yellow Pages.'

'And what's the Bankers Almanac when it's at home?'

'A big red book that lists all the banks, including the foreign ones. I used to look it up when I worked in the City.'

'You never told me you worked in the City?'

Mrs S. smiled sadly.

'It was a long time ago,' she sighed, 'before I married Mr Szaranski. A real City gent, he was. Left me at home counting the pennies while he spent the pounds on another young lady.'

For a moment, I thought the old girl was going to break down and cry but she soon bucked up and wiped her nose.

'You take my word for it,' she sniffed. 'With all your money, you can bank where you like – even with the Russians.'

The more I thought of it, the more I liked the idea. I could play Frank's little game, shunting loot from one account to another and waiting for some clown who couldn't add up to write me a nasty letter. I could even join the international set. I didn't fancy a Russian bank (well, you never knew when they might privatise them) but I could have a frog bank, a kraut bank, an Argy bank, a Yank bank (on second thoughts, Yank banks always seemed the first to go under), a wog bank, an Aussie bank. The possibilities were endless. All we needed was the Bankers' Almanac.

'Where can we get hold of a copy?' I asked.

'At the library. They're bound to have one.'

'Right. We'll go there first thing in the morning, before the spending cuts being to bite.'

To cut a long story short, I can tell you that finding a bank with the right blend of mystery and prestige is not the easiest thing in the world. After making a list, and crossing off those that looked as if they might have got their licence by mistake, we ended up with a dozen or so that looked like a miniature United Nations. Then we had to tramp round to each of them and try to open an account.

I don't know what it is about bankers but it doesn't matter what nationality they are they look at you as though you're something the cat's brought in. You'd think that somebody – an honest citizen, without a stain on his character – who walked in with a hundred grand would be welcomed with open arms. Oh, no. You could see their little eyes narrow as they focussed on Mrs S. and her shopping bag.

'I hope you don't mind my asking, sir, but this is not Liechtenstein, you understand? The money has been acquired legitimately, I suppose?'

By the time we had arrived at the Royal Bank of Jordan and explained for the umpteenth time just what the football pools were and how, if you were lucky enough to win, you ended up first in the police court, charged with assault, and then in the City looking for somewhere to deposit your winnings, I was getting a bit tired of bloody foreigners and their loaded questions. For two pins, I'd have opened an account with the TSB and been done with it.

'If you wanted the TSB, we could have opened an account in Fulham,' observed Mrs S. helpfully.

Do you know, it took two full days to find enough bankers willing to accept my money? Even then, with a hundred grand under lock and key, they wouldn't issue a cheque book until the 'necessary formalities' had been completed. Just as well we had sixty eight thousand under the mattress or we'd have been strapped for cash.

Looking back, I suppose we must have appeared an odd couple, Mrs S. and I, wandering around the City in our West End gear. Not many leather jackets outside the Bank of England, I can tell you. All top hats and rolled umbrellas. As I say, we probably drew attention to ourselves. My habit of pulling out a fifty pound note every time we stopped for a drink obviously didn't help. In the City, apparently, it's not the done thing to flaunt your wealth.

About half way through our second day, I noticed this fellah with a pink carnation in his buttonhole who seemed to be following us. Well, not exactly following; he just seemed to turn up where we were, if you know what I mean. He was even at the savoury counter at Balls Bros. when we dropped in for a bite to eat.

'I think he fancies you,' I said to Mrs S. as we struggled through the dish of the day.

'It's not me he fancies,' replied Mrs S. scowling in the direction of the quiche platter, 'but you, love. He'd fancy anybody with money.'

'You don't think he's from Interpol – or the Inland Revenue?'

'The Revenue, maybe. But you've got nothing to worry about. The football pools are tax free.'

I don't know whether the guy heard that or not but, blow me!, if he didn't walk right over to our table. Mrs S. glowered at him and, for a moment, I had a horrible feeling that Balls Bros. was about to be the centre of a new affray.

'I hope you don't mind my asking,' said our new acquaintance, hoisting himself upon a stool, 'but weren't you the chap on television the other night?'

'Doing what?' demanded Mrs S. before I had a chance to reply.

'Well, as a matter of fact, you didn't seem to be doing much at all. Just sort of sitting back and enjoying it.'

'That was me, all right,' I said before Mrs S. could get her oar in. 'At Claridge's.'

'The Dorchester, I thought it was,' 'demurred our companion. 'I go there quite a lot myself.'

'Really?'

'Yes. I'm great friends with the owner. Awfully nice chap. Lives in the Far East, you know.'

I didn't know but I didn't want to reveal my ignorance. In the City, it's not what you know, but who you know.

'Are you in the hotel business?' I asked.

'Good Lord, no!' he laughed. 'I'm sort of . . . well, just something in the City.'

He drained his glass and twiddled it nervously between his finger and thumb.

'Can I get you another one?' I asked.

'That's awfully kind of you, old boy,' he said. 'Just a little one. The claret will do.'

'How about you, Mrs S?'

'A black coffee will do very nicely, thank you,' she replied.

If looks could kill, the guy would have been stone dead by now. At the very least, his claret would have withered on the vine. I hoped that Mrs S. would not feel compelled to display her martial arts while I queued up at the bar. Amazingly, they were both still in one piece when I returned.

'I was just saying to your mother . . . ' the guy began, and I saw the muscles tense in Mrs S.'s face.

'Oh, this is not my mother,' I said hurriedly. 'This is my landlady, Mrs Szaranski.'

'Oh, I'm awfully sorry,' said our friend, taking his claret. 'I thought . . . '

'Never mind what you thought,' said Mrs S., cutting him short. 'What's your name, by the way?'

'My name? Oh, it's Jones. Freddy Jones.'

'Well, Mr Jones . . . '

'Oh, please call me Freddy,' said Freddy, raising his glass.

'Well, Mr Jones,' persisted Mrs S., 'I may not be his Mum but I am his loco in parenthesis. I am here to protect him.'

'He doesn't look to me the sort of young man who needs

much protection,' said Freddy, discussing me as though I wasn't there. 'I should have thought he could look after himself, all right.'

'Oh, he can look after himself, all right. It's his bank balance I'm protecting.'

'Oh, I see!' said Freddy. 'That sort of protection! And I thought you said you were not one of the family?'

'Now, look,' I said, just in case they had forgotten me. 'Let's not get steamed up over lunch. We've come here for a bite to eat, not to discuss the protection racket.'

'All the same,' conceded Freddy, 'your landlady does have a point. A young man in your position ought to protect his assets. How much did you say you'd won?'

'I didn't,' I replied. 'But it was in all the papers. Nearly a million.'

'Six figures, eh?' mused Freddy. 'That would certainly take some looking after.'

'Oh, it's pretty safe,' I replied. 'I put it all in the bank.'

'I hope you screwed a decent rate of interest out of them for a deposit that size?'

'Interest? No, I put it all on current account.'

Freddy seemed genuinely surprised. He put down his glass and drew closer.

'Forgive me, old boy, I know it's none of my business, but you did say you had nearly a million on current account and not earning a penny interest?'

Something about his manner made me feel very naive. Even Mrs S. looked a trifle intimidated.

'Well,' I began, 'I thought I'd have a variety of accounts so that I could have a different cheque book for every day of the week.'

'You can have a cheque book for every day of the month, if you like,' said Freddy. 'But you don't pay a million quid into the bank and expect nothing in return. Now, you take my advice. Get on to them straight away and demand a decent rate of interest, not this notional stuff they try to fob you off with. Bloody cheek!' he added, downing half his claret. 'Just like a bank to take advantage of somebody else's windfall.'

'We'll give them a ring as soon as we get home,' said Mrs S., appreciating the gravity of the situation. 'How much do you think we should ask for?'

'As much as they'll give you,' advised Freddy. 'Plus a bit for not telling you. Tell you what,' he added, 'why not come round to my office and phone from there? The sooner you get on to them, the sooner your money will begin to work for you.'

'That's awfully kind of you,' I said, slipping unconsciously into the Balls Bros. lingo. 'But I don't want to put you to any trouble.'

'No trouble at all,' said Freddy.

He took out his pocket calculator and looked at me expectantly.

'How much did you say you had?'

I told him. His face darkened.

'It'll cost you £172 just to leave that money on current account overnight. Now, drink up. There's not a moment to lose.'

Well, I could see that even Mrs S. was impressed. If we hadn't have met Freddy, we could have watched our fortune gradually ebb away.

'I'm really very glad that we met you,' I said as we followed him up the stairs and into the sunshine.

'Most fortuitous,' Freddy agreed.

'Where is your office?' asked Mrs S.

'Oh, just down there,' replied Freddy, vaguely.

He seemed a bit uncertain himself for the moment. I put it down to the claret. But he soon got his bearings and we set off at a brisk trot down Cheapside. Suddenly, we turned into a maze of narrow alleys behind St Mary-le-Bow.

'These are the original Bow bells,' said Freddy, by way of explanation. 'If you could hear these when you were born, you qualify as a Cockney.'

'That rules me out,' I said. 'I was born in the Mile End Road.'

I must say, I was a little taken aback when we arrived at Freddy's office. It was in a seedy old building that looked as though it had been built soon after the Great Fire (perhaps even before) and might still harbour the plague. Freddy bounded up the stairs to the first floor and opened the door. A couple of birds were sitting at the desk – one of them was actually sitting on it – smoking. Two empty glasses stood within reach. With a quick jerk of his head, Freddy indicated that it was time for them to leave. Then he flung open the window to let out the smoke.

'Sorry we're in such a mess,' he said. 'The decorators are downstairs and we all have to work in one room, more or less.'

'I didn't see any painters,' said Mrs S., clearly not impressed with this explanation.

'Round the back, my dear, round the back.'

Freddy cleared a space on the desk and put the telephone conspicuously in front of me.

'There we are, old boy. Now, dial away and don't take no for an answer.'

'Only one problem,' I said. 'I don't know the numbers.'

To be honest, I couldn't even remember the names of all the banks. Nine of them, all signed up within the last thirty-six hours, were more than enough for anybody to remember. As usual, Mrs S. came to the rescue. She grabbed the phone book and began flicking through the pages. Freddy hadn't got an S-Z so we had to dial directory enquiries. You need a lot of patience for that, though, so we left one bank for a personal visit.

The eight managers I was able to contact all turned out to be very reasonable. They apologised for not having explained their tariff structure and promised to transfer the funds immediately to a high-interest cheque account. At the end of an hour, I was £150 a day better off. And due entirely to Freddy.

'I really am most grateful,' I said. 'I could have lost a bomb without your advice.'

'Think nothing of it, old boy,' said Freddy, glancing anxiously towards the staircase. 'Glad to have been of assistance.'

'If there's anything I can ever do for you, just let me know.'

'I shall, I shall,' promised Freddy, ushering us, rather hurriedly, I thought, towards the door. 'Now, if you'll excuse me, I really must find out what the market has been doing.'

In my new role as a bloated plutocrat, I had quite forgotten that other folk had to work for a living. In fact, it was only when the boss phoned on the Monday following my win, demanding to know where the hell I was, that I realised I was no longer a wage slave. He seemed a bit put out when I told him what to do with his job. Technically, I suppose, I am now self-employed.

'That was a stroke of luck, running into Freddy like that,' I said, as we took the Tube back to Fulham. 'It's not every day that somebody in the City will go out of his way to advise you.'

Mrs S. said nothing. I knew she didn't like Freddy, and the two birds in his office had probably put her nose out of joint. Maybe she was just battling with feminine intuition.

As we pulled into Westminster, she said suddenly: 'If you ask me, he's nothing but a conman.'

'A conman? Who? Freddy?'

'Yes, Freddy, a conman,' she replied, quivering with emotion. 'You'll have to watch him, if you want to hold on to your million.'

'Don't be silly!' I said. 'If it wasn't for Freddy, I'd be losing money now.'

'He doesn't even know what makes a Cockney,' she said. 'And, as for that office! Well! I know office space is expensive but anybody worth his salt could afford better than that.'

'You've got a suspicious mind,' I told her. 'Anyway, I don't suppose we'll see him again.'

'I wouldn't be too sure about that,' said Mrs S.

I could see that the old girl was getting a bit stroppy. I suppose she didn't like the idea of Freddy becoming my financial adviser. After all, it was her idea to look in the Bankers' Alamanac. All Freddy could offer were three volumes of the London telephone directory.

'Tell you what,' I said, giving her a playful hug, 'why don't I buy a car and run you down to the coast? You'll feel much better for a day out.'

'I feel perfectly all right as I am,' said Mrs S. 'Besides, aren't you forgetting something?'

'What's that?'

'You can't drive.'

'All right. We'll hire a limousine. Get somebody to drive us there.'

'What's wrong with the train? asked Mrs S.

'Nothing,' I said, beginning to wish that I hadn't mentioned the sea. 'But we'll go first class. How about that?'

'All right,' said Mrs S. 'Just this once.'

By the time we reached home, I was shattered. Mentally and physically exhausted. It was a new experience.

'I think I'll have a quick kip before tea,' I informed Mrs S. as she let us in and closed the door. 'I'm knackered.'

'I'm not surprised,' said Mrs S. 'All this excitement – it takes it out of you. You put your feet up and I'll make a nice cup of tea.'

I had no sooner put my head on the pillow than I was asleep. But with the old adrenalin pumping round the system like molasses under pressure I was awake before Mrs S. knocked at the door with a pot of tea. Best silver teapot, too, I noticed. And a huge slice of Black Forest gateau.

'Now, Mrs S., you mustn't spoil me!' I protested. 'A cup of tea and a chocolate biscuit would have done just as well.'

'What's the point of having money if you can't enjoy it?' asked Mrs S., arranging the tray on the bedside table. 'Anyway, I thought you would be hungry.'

As I was about to pour, there was a tremendous hammering on the front door. I looked at Mrs S. She looked at me. I thought of the money under the mattress. By the look on her face, so did she.

'It's all right, I'll go,' I said, trying not to let my natural cowardice get the better of me. 'It's probably only the bank manager come to return my old cheques.'

'No, you stay there and enjoy your tea,' said Mrs S., recovering her poise. 'I'll sort him out.'

I heard her trot down the stairs and open the front door. An exchange of greetings was followed by hurried footsteps on the stairs. Frank burst into the room. His eyes rested on the gateau.

'So this is how the rich live?' he remarked.

'What's up, sport?' I said, stirring my tea. 'You look all hot and bothered.'

'I am,' said Frank, sitting on the bed. 'it's this no-good,

goddam, lousy country.'

'Oh, I don't know. It's not such a bad place, once you get used to it.'

'It's okay if you're rich. Property prices going up every day, taxes coming down. But, if you're skint, like me – and like you was last week – it's not so hot.'

'Have a bite of gateau,' I said.

'No, thanks.'

'Cuppa tea?'

'No.'

'Well, you didn't come here to discuss property prices.'

Frank shifted uncomfortably on the bed. His eyes avoided mine – not like Freddy's, whose little orbs fixed you like a stoat sizing up a rabbit. He was obviously trying to summon up courage.

'How much do you want?' I asked.

'Honest, Sid, you know I wouldn't touch you for a quid unless I was desperate. But I gotta get away before I end up in the loony bin.'

'I know the feeling,' I said.

'What I'd like,' said Frank, 'is to go to Australia, like we were talking about last week. You remember?'

'Sure, I remember.'

'I'm not asking for a gift, just a loan to tide me over till I've got a job and settled in. I'll pay you back, with interest. I promise.'

'No sweat,' I said. 'I'll just have a word with the bank manager.'

'You're a sport, Sid.'

'Mrs S!' I called. 'Could you have a look under the mattress and bring me up a thousand quid?' I turned to Frank. 'That enough to be going on with?'

'More than enough,' said Frank. 'I could go first-class for that.'

'Yeah, well, you don't want to arrive looking like a ten-pound Pom on the run from the bailiffs. Where you going? Sydney?'

'Thought I might,' said Frank, looking much happier than

when he came in. 'Paradise for the working classes, they reckon. Like Russia, with sunshine.'

Mrs S. seemed to be taking her time getting the money. Maybe she was having trouble lifting the mattress. Eventually, she climbed the stairs and stomped into the room. I could tell that Frank was about as welcome as a ratcatcher with Aids.

'One thousand pounds,' she said, handing over the money very purposefully to me. 'Exactly. In fifty-pound notes.'

'Thanks, Mrs S.,' I said. 'Frank here is leaving the country in a bit of a hurry.'

'And you're lending him money?'

'Why not? He's only going to Australia, aren't you, mate?'

'Too right,' said Frank, exercising his new vowels.

Mrs S. cast her eyes heavenwards and stomped out of the room. Her faith in Frank was not as great as mine. I had drunk with him, exchanged cheques with him and faced the wrath of bank managers with him. You couldn't expect a woman to understand things like that.

'When you off, then?' I asked, finishing the gateau and squeezing another cup from the pot.

'Tomorrow, if I can get a seat,' said Frank.

'Not in trouble with the law, are you?'

'No, but I could be in about nine months, if you see what I mean.'

'Well, you're a dark horse!' I cried. 'You never told me you had a bird.'

' A one-night stand, after we'd been watching those condom ads. on the telly. Put us in the mood.'

'Pity you didn't use one,' I said, standing up and shaking the crumbs on to the floor. 'There you are, old son. One thousand smackers. Don't worry about the repayments. Just send a bit on account, when you can.'

'Thanks, Sid. You're a real pal. I won't forget you.'

'You must be out of your mind!' snapped Mrs S. when Frank had gone. 'Fancy lending a thousand quid to a bloke on the way to a convict colony! I wouldn't mind betting he's stolen a few sheep in his time, too.'

'What's a grand when you've got a million? Old Frank

deserves a break. Good luck to him.'

Mrs S. sniffed huffily. First the begging letters, now the personal friends en route to the antipodes. At that moment the telephone rang.

'It's for you,' she said. 'That Freddy fellah. I told you we hadn't heard the last of him.'

'Sshh!' I said, putting my hand over the receiver. 'He'll hear you.'

'And a jolly good thing, too. Might learn some home truths.'

I sat down to take the call. How had he got the number? That's what I wanted to know.

'Hullo, Sid, old boy,' warbled our City friend. 'Hope you got home all right, without incident?'

'I wasn't mugged, if that's what you mean.'

Freddy chuckled.

'Sorry I had to leave you in the lurch, so to speak, but I had to get in touch with my broker. As a matter of fact, I did mention our meeting to him. I hope you don't mind?'

'Not at all,' I said. 'What sort of broker is he?'

'Oh, just the ordinary sort. Only deals in a small way but I always think you get a better service from a small firm, don't you?'

'I don't know,' I confessed. 'I've never had much to do with brokers.'

'Really? You do surprise me.'

Mrs S., who had her ear to the phone, was looking daggers drawn.

'Actually,' continued Freddy, 'I was wondering whether you'd like to meet him over a spot of lunch? You never know, he might well be of assistance to you.'

'I don't see why not,' I said, ignoring Mrs S. 'What day do you suggest?'

'Tomorrow?' said Freddy.

'Tomorrow's Saturday. And, in any case, we're going to Brighton.'

'Isn't that extraordinary!' exclaimed Freddy. 'We were both planning to go there ourselves tomorrow. Some clients at Roedean, you know. Why don't we all meet at the Pavilion at about half twelve and find a little eatery somewhere?'

'Sounds all right to me,' I said. 'See you under the Dome at half twelve.'

'Super!' said Freddy. 'It's on me, by the way.'

I turned to Mrs S.

'We're going to have company for lunch tomorrow. Freddy wants to introduce his broker.'

She received the news without enthusiasm. I could see that Freddy was going to have to brush up his personal interface.

'I hope you enjoyed your gateau?' asked Mrs S.

'Oh, yes. Very nice, thank you.'

'Good,' she said, and disappeared into her room.

3. Inside information

Some bloke wrote a book about Brighton. Brighton Rock, I think it was called. All about punks and vitriol. You don't hear much about vitriol these days. Overtaken by technology, I expect. Still plenty of punks, though. Hundreds of 'em, stretched out on the pebbles, in pairs. Bit off-putting, really. I don't know why they can't go to Spain for that sort of thing.

The guard on the train down had an old-fashioned touch of vitriol about him. I guess he didn't expect to find the likes of us in a first-class compartment, even though Mrs S. was looking very smart in a gipsy-type outfit unearthed from her bottom drawer.

'Won the pools, then?' he asked, holding up our tickets to the light.

'No, we're friends of Ernie's,' replied Mrs S., a bit sharpish. 'And the chairman's.'

'Have a nice day,' the guard said, closing the door.

'Bloody cheek!' exclaimed Mrs S. 'Just because he's got a British Rail pass.'

As I have already hinted, the beach at Brighton is not much to look at. All pebbles and pollution. I was looking for the blue flag but all I could see was an advertisement for the dry cleaners. So, after a quick shufti and a lungful of sea air, we strolled towards the Pavilion. Strange looking place, almost oriental. I wondered if it was anything to do with Freddy's friend at the Dorchester. Apparently not. The guy on the door said it was built by the Prince Regent, whoever he was.

Freddy was looking up at the pigeons when we spotted him. He wore a grey, pin-striped suit, brown Homburg and carried an umbrella. I hoped he wasn't expecting rain. Standing next to him was a chubby fellah of about the same age but with a different tailor. His stripes were much broader than Freddy's, the sort you normally find in a second-hand car showroom. Freddy waved cheerfully as we approached.

'Good morning, madam,' he said, taking Mrs S.'s hand and

pressing it softly to his lips. 'You're looking very well. Good trip?'

'So far,' said Mrs S.

'Allow me to introduce my friend, Bernie,' Freddy continued. 'The best, most efficient, broker in the business.'

Bernie extended a podgy hand. It was a bit moist but the grip was firm enough.

'How long have you been a member of the Stock Exchange?' I asked.

'Oh, well, as a matter of fact . . . '

'Let's go and have a bite to eat,' said Freddy, looking at his watch. 'I know a nice little place not far from here. In fact, I've taken the liberty of booking a table. I hope that's all right?'

'That's fine by me,' I said. 'Lead on.'

I expect you've seen one of those old Hollywood movies where the Mob suddenly appears from under a table in a high-class Sicilian joint and mows down everybody in sight. That's what the Trattoria del Duce reminded me of. A bit like a film set, only twice as expensive. I was glad that Freddy was paying.

'Freddy tells me that you've come into money?' said Bernie, as we nibbled our hors d'oeuvres.

'Just a little,' I said.

'I wouldn't call a million quid little.'

'Depends what you're used to, I suppose,' chipped in Mrs S.

Bernie raised an eyebrow and exchanged glances with our host.

'Put it this way,' he said. 'It sounds quite a useful amount.'

'Very useful,' I said. 'Thanks to Freddy, it's all in the bank, earning a decent rate of interest.'

'Ah, but there's the rub,' said Bernie. 'I don't want to suggest that you've done the wrong thing. But, by taking the interest, you are gradually eating your capital. Do you follow?'

Well, even I could see that, as prices went up and my bank balance didn't, sooner or later my million would be worth about tuppence h'penny.

'What you must do is get into growth stocks,' said Bernie.

'Growth stocks?'

'Yes, shares that will grow in value and make you happy in

your old age.'

'I'd like to be happy before then,' I said.

Mrs S., crunching her celery, was listening carefully. She didn't trust Bernie, that's for sure, but as far as I could see he was talking good sense. Money had to be invested properly, if you were not to end up broke. It was no good just leaving it in the bank – which was against my natural instincts, anyway.

'What you need,' said Freddy, as the waiter uncorked a bottle of Roussillon '86, 'is somebody you can turn to for advice. Somebody with his finger on the pulse.'

Bernie caught my eye.

'I'd be more than happy to accept you as a client,' he said. 'I won't even ask for a banker's reference – ha-ha!'

Mrs S. was tearing into her rump steak like a tiger with the first kill of the day.

'I don't think Mr Arbuthnot wants to fritter away his fortune on the Stock Exchange,' she said. 'If he wants to gamble, he can go to the races.'

'My dear madam,' said Bernie gently, 'investing in stocks and shares is not gambling. As I've just explained, you can't sit back and allow your capital to be eroded by inflation. That's the route to the poorhouse.'

'I suppose you charge for your advice?' said Mrs S., attacking from a different quarter.

'Certainly not,' said Bernie, stuffing half a dozen pommes des frites down his gullet. 'Of course, we charge commission; even stockbrokers have to live.'

'Some of them live too well, if you ask me,' said Mrs S.

'I think you'll find,' said Freddy, 'that there's a scale of charges that applies to everybody, more or less.'

'And of course,' added Bernie, 'you'll get all the benefits of our research department.'

'Research department?'

'Yes. We don't just say to clients, buy this or sell that. We make a few enquiries before recommending a share. Investment should not be a matter of guesswork.'

'And what do you recommend at the moment?'

Bernie glanced around, as though half expecting to find a

rival broker – or perhaps a man with a machine gun – lurking under the sweet trolley.

'Strictly entre nous,' he confided, 'we were having lunch the other day with the chairman of a little company up North, weren't we, old boy?'

'Indeed,' Freddy confirmed. 'Very interesting situation there, if you ask me. Fraught with possibilities.'

'Almost begging to be taken over,' said Bernie.

'Certainly scope for upside potential,' Freddy agreed.

'Does that mean I ought to buy some shares?' I asked.

'I shouldn't think you'd get another chance to buy them at this level,' said Bernie, 'especially if a bidder comes out of the woodwork.'

'How much are they?' I asked.

'Eleven pence,' said Bernie.

'If it's such a good company, why are the shares only eleven pee?' demanded Mrs S.

'Very often,' explained Freddy patiently, 'shares get over-looked because investors chase more fashionable stocks, like Japanese hi-tech industries. Nobody wants to know about Christmas puddings any more.'

'Is that what it does? Makes Christmas puddings?'

'And very successfully, too,' said Bernie. 'You mark my words, when the accounts are published there's going to be some action there.'

I prodded the remains of my jambon sicilienne. Bit of gristle there, I thought, but I won't complain. The film set might erupt.

'I've never owned any shares before,' I confessed.

'There's a first time for everything, eh?' laughed Freddy, casting an admiring glance at Mrs S.

'Do you know,' said Bernie, bringing the conversation back to the Christmas-pudding level, 'before the present lot came to power' – I assumed he meant the government – 'hardly anybody owned shares. Now you can't get on a bus without somebody accosting you about their British Telecom.'

'I wonder why nobody bought shares, say, ten years ago.'

'Probably too stupid to know what was good for them,' said

Bernie.

'Perhaps they had read about the Great Crash of 1929?' suggested Mrs S., revealing a surprising knowledge of financial history.

Freddy laughed.

'That was a once-in-a-lifetime affair. We won't see anything like that again.'

'That's all right, then,' said Mrs S. 'I wouldn't want Mr Arbuthnot to lose all his money.'

'Don't you worry your pretty head over that,' said Freddy, making what I thought was a fairly ill-disguised pass at Mrs S. 'Just you leave it to us and Sid's fortune will get bigger and bigger.'

'Well,' I said, sensing that they were expecting me to say something, 'do you think I ought to invest a few quid in this Christmas-pudding outfit?'

'You could do a lot worse,' said Bernie. 'And, if all goes according to plan, you could do very well.'

'According to plan?' I said.

Bernie looked embarrassed.

'A slip of the tongue, old boy. What I meant was that, even if the takeover fails to materialise, seasonal factors will adjust the share price.'

'I think,' said Freddy, lowering his voice, 'that if Sid is to put some money into Northern Puds we should tell him the whole story.'

'I thought there was more to it than met the eye,' said Mrs S., who now resembled a slightly tipsy gipsy.

'My dear lady, you mustn't have such a suspicious mind,' said Freddy. 'The fact is that when we had lunch with the chairman last week he let slip that the company was well into the black now and the market would be pleasantly surprised when the figures were announced.'

'In the black?' I said. 'You mean, it has been in the red?'

'The pudding sector has, as I expect you know, been getting rather a bad Press just lately. All this twaddle about healthy living. I do wish that wretched woman would shut up. You'd think Northerners were the only people to suffer from cardiovascular disease.'

'In fact,' said Bernie, 'our market research has shown that most people couldn't give a stuff about what they eat. And, of course, that's very good for sales. It's just a question of image, really.'

I could see that to be an investor one had to have a grasp of politics, as well as economics.

'And so it hasn't been easy,' said Bernie. 'But as far as this little outfit is concerned the worst is well and truly over.'

'Maybe I ought to buy a couple of thousand, then?'

'A couple of thousand? My dear chap, you wouldn't find a broker willing to buy you that amount. You've got to think big. A couple of million would be more like it.'

I tried to remember what that wretched woman had also said about alcohol impairing the mental faculties. I couldn't, which must have proved it, I suppose. But two million shares seemed a hell of a lot to me.

'What sort of income can I expect from them?' I asked.

'Well, they don't exactly pay a dividend at the moment,' said Freddy, 'for reasons I've already explained. But, in any case, you're not buying for income but for capital gain.'

'Once they've put on a few pence, you can sell 'em again,' added Bernie.

How did the saying go? 'You've got to speculate to accumulate'. The old brain sifted through the cliches. 'A fool and his money are soon parted'. They couldn't both be right. Anyway, I was no fool. I glanced at Freddy. He was smiling at Mrs S. I considered the facts. Here was I, dining at a posh restaurant in Brighton with my new broker, surrounded by Sicilian gentlemen who looked as though they might require a large tip, and contemplating my first steps along the road of popular capitalism. I had a strange feeling that something was gnawing at the butt of my cheque book. I glanced at Bernie. He was picking his teeth.

'All right,' I said, opting to speculate. 'I'll try half a million. But make sure you don't pay more than you have to.'

'Leave it to me, old boy,' said Bernie. 'We're used to the market. Softly, softly, catchee monkey.'

'What do you want to catch a monkey for?' asked Mrs S. taking a renewed interest in the conversation. 'I thought we were buying Christmas puddings?'

'Figure of speech, dear lady,' replied Bernie. 'What I meant was that we won't rush in where angels fear to tread. No point in tipping off everybody that there's a willing buyer.'

'Why not?' asked Mrs S.

'Because they'd all ditch their shares, that's why. As a matter of fact,' he continued, 'I think I know where I can get hold of one or two without alerting the market. Might have to pay a penny or two more, though.'

'So long as it's only a penny or two,' I warned.

'Leave it to me, old boy. As soon as the market opens, I'll be in there, scrabbling on your behalf.' He glanced at his watch. 'Now, if you don't mind, we'll be getting back to London. Lot of paper work to catch up on over the weekend. I'll be glad when this privatisation nonsense is over.'

Freddy signalled to one of the Sicilians to bring l'addizione. He fumbled in his wallet and finally produced a credit card.

'I'm a-sorry, sir, but we do not-a take this card,' said the chief mafioso, with a smile that sent a shiver down my spine.

'Here,' I said, moving swiftly to defuse an embarrassing situation, 'have this one on me.'

I pulled out a handful of notes and placed them on the little dish. The mafioso looked much happier.

'That's awfully kind of you, old boy,' said Freddy. 'I really do apologise. I had no idea they were allergic to plastic.'

'Don't worry about it,' I said. 'I owe you a favour, anyway.'

They stood up to take their leave. Bernie extended a podgy hand. It was a bit greasy now as well as moist.

'I'm so glad we've met,' he said. 'Half a million Northern Puds, at best. It's as good as done.'

And with that they were gone. Mrs S., clutching her bag, disappeared in the direction of the ladies' room. I sat down and waited idly for her return. I glanced at the bill again. The Sussex mafiosi had nothing to learn from the folks back home. The chief brigand was hovering ominously in the background.

'Can I bring you something to drink while you are waiting,

signor?'

Well, why not? The thought of tramping along the front, admiring the pier and avoiding the candy floss, was not one to lift the spirits naturally.

'I'll have a glass of champagne,' I said.

'I'm afraid we don't serve champagne by the glass, sir.'

'Righty-o. Bring me a bottle.'

'Si, signor.'

By the time Mrs S. returned, I was three sheets to the wind and feeling pretty pleased with myself. Not only was I a shareholder (or would be, as soon as the market opened on Monday), but I knew more about Northern Puds than almost anybody in London. I bet not everybody who bought shares for the first time did so on the basis of such thorough research.

'Inside information,' said Mrs S., pouring cold water on my euphoria. 'You can go to jail for that.'

'Jail? What, for listening to my broker over lunch?'

'Not for listening but for buying shares on the strength of what he says. I'd keep quiet about it, if I were you.'

The champagne came to fifteen quid. I'd have been better off with a stubby among the seagulls. I gave the waiter twenty pounds and hoped he wouldn't forget Mama in Sicily.

'We'll have to order the F.T. next week,' I said, as we journeyed back to London. 'You never know, the shares could take off if somebody makes a bid for them.'

The bloke in the corner sat up with a start. He had been pretending to read The Economist but, in fact, was resting his eyes. I guess that's the effect The Economist has on you, especially on a Saturday afternoon.

'Yes,' I continued, letting the champagne do the talking, 'I wouldn't be at all surprised if the Russians bought a stake in the old Christmas pud company. They go in for stodgy stuff. Helps to keep out the cold.'

'The Russians don't believe in shares,' said Mrs S. 'They've got more sense.'

'Oh, yes?' I said. 'What about all those lampshades in the Portobello Road? They were supposed to have been made out of genuine Russian share certificates.'

'I still can't see them investing in Christmas puds,' said Mrs S., 'especially at eleven pee a time.'

'Twenty pee, by the end of the week, if we're lucky.'

The bloke in the corner pretended to go back to sleep again but as we pulled into Victoria he was up like a shot. Grabbing his Filofax, he smiled faintly and hurried towards the barrier. I imagine he had been travelling on a second-class ticket and didn't want us to see.

We spent a pretty anxious weekend, I can tell you, once the effect of the champagne had worn off. I could see why financiers got ulcers, worrying about their shares all the time. And I hadn't even got mine yet. By the time Monday morning arrived, I was in a bit of a state.

'For goodness' sake, stop worrying,' said Mrs S. 'If you go on like this, you'll be a nervous wreck.'

At lunchtime, the phone rang.

'Hullo, Sid?'

Freddy, not Bernie.

'Thought I'd just give a ring to say that everything is under control. We're trying to put together a parcel without spilling the beans. Don't want the price to gallop ahead just yet, eh?'

'Not until I've got them, eh?'

'Quite,' said Freddy.

On Tuesday morning, Mrs S. went to the corner shop and got hold of a copy of The Times. (We had decided against the F.T.; too technical for a first-time buyer.) We spread it out on the kitchen table and looked for a reference to Northern Puds. Not a word. The shares weren't even listed.

'You don't think . . . ?' I began.

'That you've been sold a pup?'

'Looks a bit odd, doesn't it?'

'Well, you haven't written out a cheque yet so you can't have lost anything.'

'No, but what about this thing, "My word is my bond"? I told Bernie I would buy them. I can't back out now.'

'Why not give him a ring? Insist on your right to know.'

It was then that I realised that I hadn't got Bernie's telephone number. I didn't even know the name of his firm. I was on to

Freddy pretty smartish.

'By the way,' I said, 'I can't find the shares listed in the paper. Why's that?'

'Well,' said Freddy, clearing his throat, 'the papers don't print everything, of course. If you want to know everything that has been traded you'll need the Official List. But that's frightfully boring. I wouldn't bother, if I were you. Just hang on and you'll see Christmas puds in the paper soon enough.'

He was right, Goddammit! The following morning, that chap who writes the market column in the Daily Mail had picked up a rumour.

'Listen to this!' I cried, reading aloud to Mrs S. 'Rumours that Northern Puds, the troubled confectioner, had pulled off an export deal with the Russians helped the shares put on 2p at 13p.'

'Is that all?' asked Mrs S.

'Two pee is two pee,' I reminded her.

'No, I meant, is that the end of the story?'

'Well, it's a hundred per cent more than yesterday. I wonder why he didn't mention the takeover?'

'Probably doesn't know about it yet,' said Mrs S.

Not privy to inside information, I thought.

By the next day, The Times and a couple of other papers were on to it. The Times said that speculation that a bidder was trying to acquire a stake in Northern Puds had pushed up the shares another 2p to 14p.

'I don't get it,' I said. 'If they were 13p yesterday and they put on another 2p, they ought to be 15p.'

'Different paper,' explained Mrs S.

'You'd think they'd be more expensive in The Times than in the Mail.'

'You pays your money and takes your choice,' said Mrs S.

By Thursday, even the Daily Smut had cottoned on to the fact that something was stirring in Northern Puds.

'Guess what, folks!' it shrieked. 'The Perestroika Pud is on the way. Yes, the Ruskies' favourite brekky food group is about to be taken over. By the Ruskies!!! Northern Puds, which has been painting the Dales red with its accounts, has been given the come-on by the Kremlin. A whole drosky load of roubles is said to be on the way. Good for glasnost! Good for us! Fill your boots now, folks, before it's too late.'

'That's more like it,' I said to Mrs S. as the price crept up to 17p. 'What's half a million sixpences?'

At lunchtime, Bernie himself came on the line.

'We've managed to complete your order, old boy,' he said. 'Half a million Northern Puds. I must say, the market seems to be taking a renewed interest in the stock.'

'Has it been taken over yet?' I asked.

Bernie chuckled.

'Not by the Russians,' he said.

So much for the Perestroika Pud, I thought.

'How much am I making so far?' I asked.

The question seemed to take Bernie by surprise. There was a short pause, presumably while he was plugging in his electronic calculator.

'I don't think we should talk about profit just yet,' he cautioned. 'After all, shares are for long-term growth, not short-term gain.'

'But if I bought at eleven pence and they're now sixteen pence, I'm at least five pee a share to the good.'

Bernie coughed.

'Unfortunately,' he said, 'we weren't able to get all the shares at the lower price. We managed to get a handful at twelve but I'm afraid we had to pay fourteen or fifteen for the balance.'

'So that means I'm not making any money yet?'

'Let's say you've probably covered the commission.'

'Commission?'

'My commission, for buying them.'

'I see.'

'I'll send you a contract note at the end of the account and you'll see precisely how much you owe me. The main thing is that the order has been completed.'

Mrs S. was sceptical, to say the least.

'So, you won't know how much you paid and how much you've made till the end of the account, whenever that might be. I just hope they continue to go up.'

For some reason, Northern Puds didn't go up any more that week. Instead, the dipped to 14p and stayed there, refusing to budge. The Daily Smut, which had been so fulsome in its praise a few days earlier, was strangely silent. Only the guy on the Mail, who is supposed to reach parts of the market that lesser hacks are unable to reach, managed to squeeze in a line.

'The Stock Exchange is investigating recent dealings in Northern Puds,' he wrote. 'The buying is thought to have come mainly from one small firm of brokers.'

Freddy was on the line before the ink had dried.

'You're in the news already!' he gasped. 'First venture into the stock market and the Exchange wants to know what you're doing.'

'I haven't done anything,' I said, failing to see what all the fuss was about. 'All I've done is buy some shares.'

'Quite so,' said Freddy. 'And, if the Exchange enquires, that's all you have to say. Do you follow?'

Well, I didn't follow and the Exchange didn't enquire. At lunchtime came the news that some sheikh from Saudi Arabia with a fixation for British sweetmeats had made an offer for Northern Puds. He was apparently on the point of going home when he saw the report in the Daily Smut. Rather that let a God-fearing British company fall into the hands of the Russians he was offering thirty pence a share.

I was on to Bernie in a flash.

'Did you hear the news!' I cried. 'The bid! It's here!'

Bernie seemed to have some difficulty in speaking. His voice sounded hoarse and husky.

'So I understand,' he said, without enthusiasm.

'Shall I accept the offer or hold on for a better one?'

'I'd accept, if I were you.'

'A bird in the desert is worth two in the Dales, eh?' I remarked, wittily.

'Quite,' said Bernie.

'It's nice to make a profit,' I said, 'but I fell real sorry for the guy who sold the shares. He'd have cleaned up, if he'd hung on.'

'That's the way the cookie crumbles,' said Bernie, sadly.

4. *I just wanna be part of it*

Freddy looked a bit down in the mouth when I met him for lunch at Balls Bros. He was obviously kicking himself for not having bought any shares in Northern Puds.

'Cheer up,' I said. 'There are bound to be other takeover situations.'

'Very probably,' he said.

I had managed to shake off Mrs S. for the day. She had gone to visit her mother's grave. For years, she had reproached herself for not being able to afford a headstone. I told her to help herself from under the mattress. I mean, if a millionaire can't show some respect for the dead, he can't expect much respect from the living.

'What shall we buy next?' I asked, topping up Freddy's glass.

'With your luck, a thousand of anything.'

'What do they do?'

'Who?'

'This anything outfit.'

Freddy scratched his head. He was clearly under the weather.

'What I meant was that, if the market's going up – which appears to be the case – you could invest in more or less anything and still make money. It doesn't matter. You just follow the crowd.'

'Doesn't sound very scientific to me.'

'My dear Sid,' said Freddy, somewhat testily, 'you will never make money if you allow science to influence your decisions. The market works on emotion, not logic.'

I refrained from reminding him that I had already done rather well and that my success was based on inside information, not crowd psychology.

'What does the research department suggest?', I asked.

'They're a bit short staffed at the moment. We're relying mainly on the comment in the F.T.'

'There must be something I can buy?'

'Now I come to think of it,' said Freddy, perking up at the sight of a new bottle, 'I did hear of a little show that's going great guns in Europe.'

'The Channel Tunnel?' I guessed.

'No,' said Freddy, 'but you're not far off. Come 1992, when English hooligans will be pouring on to the Continent like the hordes of Ghengis Khan, they'll need a few maps to show 'em the way.'

'Can't they buy those now?' I asked.

'Sure,' said Freddy. 'But I think you'll find that, with the high-speed trains, the maps being drawn today will be totally out of date. Imagine thinking you were still in Calais when, in fact, you were hurtling through the Bois de Boulogne. Embarrassing, what?'

'To be quite honest, it doesn't sound very exciting to me. Anybody can make maps.'

'Ah! But these are very special maps,' said Freddy. 'They not only show where the Chunnel will be popping up on both sides of the water but they contain a whole mass of ecological information.'

'Such as?'

'Wine lakes, beef mountains, set-aside areas. Absolute must for anybody who wants to know how their taxes are spent.'

'What's the name of this outfit?' I asked.

'Euro Jaunts,' said Freddy. 'First-rate little company. Dynamic, entrepreneurial. Run by a pal of mine, actually.

'I can't see much demand for a map showing set-aside areas, whatever they are. Who'd want to buy that?'

'You'd be surprised,' said Freddy. 'I have it on good authority that anything to do with the environment is going to sell like hot cakes. The government is almost bound to snap up the entire first print run. From what I gather, they don't know their greens from their Euro sprouts half the time.'

'I'm sorry,' I said. 'I want somethng that will outperform the market.'

'You have been reading your F.T.,' said Freddy, waspishly.

'I can't afford to wait till 1992. I want something that will double my money in a couple of weeks.'

'Don't we all?' sighed Freddy.

'What about ICI, Marks and Spencer – something in the top 100 index?'

'I thought you wanted excitement?'

'It would be very exciting being part of British Petroleum,' I said.

'You don't want to get mixed up with the wogs,' said Freddy. 'Besides, B.P. is subject to fluctuations in the dollar.'

'Is that a bad thing?'

'It is if you're not a foreign exchange dealer.'

Freddy was twiddling his empty glass again. I topped it up with a flourish, just to show that we were still friends.

'I still quite like the idea of ICI,' I said. 'A good, solid British company.'

'All right,' said Freddy. 'It's your money. How many would you like?'

It's a funny thing, money. When I didn't have any, I always slept soundly at night. My overdraft was the bank manager's problem. Now I had half a million quid at risk, I was as anxious as a broody hen. B.P., Courtaulds, ICI; you name it, it was part of my portfolio. Not to mention fifty thousand Euro Jaunts that Freddy eventually persuaded me to buy.

'If you can't stand the heat, you shouldn't be in the kitchen,' said Mrs S., pouring me another cup of strong, black coffee.

So wrapped up in my own affairs was I that I had forgotten to ask how she had got on herself.

'How was Mother?' I asked, trying not to sound flippant.

'Oh, Sid!' she cried, spilling coffee all over the Daily Smut. 'I couldn't find her!'

'Couldn't find her?'

'When I got there, there was this big notice saying the graveyard had been privatised. Mother has been moved to make way for a housing estate.'

'But they can't do that!' I cried. 'It's blasphemous, that's what it is!'

'They said it was something to do with being rate-capped.'

'Rate-capped? What cobblers! It's just another of these Tory plots to flog off public assets. Don't you worry, Mrs S. We'll go down first thing tomorrow and find out what's happened.'

I could hear Mrs S. sobbing occasionally through the night. I wished I could have done something to comfort her. Even though I was a millionaire, my sympathies were still very much with the underdog. Mind you, she hadn't shown much interest in the grave over the past year or two. I suppose it was the shock of finding it gone. You know what women are like. Emotional creatures; get upset over the slightest thing. Still, the overpaid louts in the town hall had no right to remove Mother's remains without telling anybody.

The following morning we went to the town hall to demand an explanation – if necessary, backed with the threat of legal action. An old geezer who looked as if he would soon be in the grave himself led us into a side room and smiled weakly.

'I'm sorry your discovery came as such a shock,' he said to Mrs S. 'We did think that the council's decision had been widely publicised. It has been in all the papers.'

'It wasn't in the Daily Smut,' I said, 'and that is what this lady reads.'

'I think you'll find it was,' said the old gentleman, preparing to disagree. 'In fact, their story carried a particularly lurid headline.'

'Then I'm surprised I didn't see it,' I said.

'Yes,' the old gentleman continued, 'the council has been forced by economic circumstances to lease the cemetery to an oil exploration company which plans to drill a number of test holes. Hence the headline: Bored Stiffs!'

I thought Mrs S. was going to faint. Her normally chubby features became pale and gaunt. Instead, she just muttered a very feeble, 'Oh, my God!'

'I personally thought the headline was in excruciatingly bad taste,' said the old gentleman. 'But I'm afraid it reflects the values of the society in which we live – which tend to be more Philistine than Victorian.'

'What about my mother?' asked Mrs S., faintly.

'She has not been violated in any way, I can assure you. We were very strict about that. Now, what did you say her name was?'

We told him.

'Ah, yes,' he said, flicking through a sheaf of computer print-outs, 'I think you will find that Mrs Rosenbaum is perfectly safe. She has been moved to the Jewish cemetery in the neighbouring borough.'

'But she wasn't even Jewish!' cried Mrs S.

The old gentleman peered over the top of his glasses.

'With a name like that?' he smiled.

'Yes, even with a name like that!' wailed Mrs S. 'And to think of all those shillings she put in the box over the years! That's the reward she gets!'

'I'm very sorry if we have offended you,' the old gentleman said. 'I personally would not mind where I came to rest, so long as I wasn't forgotten. And, if I may be uncharitable for a moment, we did think that Mrs Rosenbaum had slipped from the memory, so to speak.'

'That's because I hadn't any money,' sobbed Mrs S., wiping a tear from her cheek. 'But now that Mr Arbuthnot has won the pools . . . '

'And made a few quid on the Stock Exchange,' I reminded her.

' . . . now that we can afford it, I wanted to do the best for Mother.'

'We could try to get her back, if you like,' the old gentleman ventured, 'although I regret to say that she would not be able to occupy her previous resting place. Personally, I would feel a lot happier in a Jewish cemetery than in a Christian one with an oil rig on top of me.'

'What happens if they don't strike oil?' I asked. 'Surely, you could pop her back in the same hole, then?'

'I'm afraid not,' the old gentleman said. 'If the rest of the drilling proves to be unsuccessful, the oil company is obliged to relinquish its lease and sell the land on to a property company.'

'Who would want to live in a graveyard?' I asked.

'It's a question of land, I'm afraid, sir. They're not making it any more.'

'Do you, by any chance, happen to know the name of the oil

company or the property developer?' I asked, hoping not to sound mercenary at a time of emotional distress.

'Phoenix Hydrocarbons and Renaissance Properties,' the old gentleman replied. 'Both traded on the over-the-counter market, I believe.'

'Schmucks!' cried Mrs S., betraying her origins. 'Both run by a bunch of schmucks!'

'I shall assume, then,' the old gentleman said, 'that you are quite happy to leave your mother in her current resting place?'

'I don't have much choice, do I?' asked Mrs S., now fully recovered. 'Just tell me the plot number and I'll weigh her down with a block of stone so big that not even a bunch of schmucks will be able to move it.'

'I think you are confusing the cemeteries, madam,' the old gentleman said.

I don't want to sound sacrilegious but I couldn't help thinking on the way home that the trip had not been entirely a waste of time. Let me rephrase that. It had certainly not been a waste of time for Mrs S. She had tracked down her long-forgotten Mum. But what about those two companies that were going to make the council's fortune? If they could reap the benefits of privatisation, then so could I. As soon as Mrs S. was out of earshot (I didn't want to upset her again), I got on the phone to Bernie.

'I've been thinking,' I said, hoping that Mrs S. would not return at the critical moment. 'I want to buy some shares in an oil well.'

'One with oil or one without?'

'No, straight up. Phoenix Hydrocarbons. They're drilling in the cemetery. You may have read it in the papers.'

'Oh, yes, I remember,' said Bernie. 'I wouldn't touch 'em with a bargepole, if I were you.'

'Really? The council is pinning its hopes on them.'

'The council? What would the council know about drilling for oil? They can't even empty the dustbins.'

'They must have thought there was a chance or they wouldn't have granted a lease.'

'You've no idea what people will do when they get into

power. They'd flog off the methane from the sewers if they thought there was an MBE in it.'

Bernie sounded very truculent. I wondered if I'd caught him at an awkward time.

'I thought it was a good two-way bet,' I said. 'If they don't strike oil, they'll build houses there.'

'That's more like it,' Bernie agreed. 'Plenty of money in bricks and mortar. Why not buy a few of those?'

'I was going to. Renaissance Properties. Can you get me fifty thousand?'

'At best?'

'No higher than yesterday's close.'

I had been caught like that before.

'Tell you what,' said Bernie, 'why not take out an option on Phoenix? If they stike oil, you win. If they don't, you only lose your stake money.'

'Sounds like gambling to me.'

'I thought you wanted a two-way bet?'

'Is that what options are all about?'

'We call it hedging,' said Bernie. 'Look at it this way. If Phoenix strikes oil, your property shares are not going to be worth very much, are they?'

'No,' I conceded.

'So you'll need something to protect your investment there. A put option, I reckon.'

'A put option?'

'Yeah. You buy the shares, right? And you also take out a put option. If the price falls, you just offload the shares on to the bloke who wrote the option.'

'But who would buy, knowing they'd make a loss?'

'The world's full of idiots,' said Bernie.

'Doesn't sound very ethical to me,' I said. 'Robbing Peter to pay Paul.'

'Listen,' said Bernie. 'Don't start worrying about the other fellah or you'll never get rich. In this game, it's every man for himself.'

'What about loving thy neighbour? Doesn't that come into it?'

'You can screw the pants off the whole street, if you like,' said Bernie. 'But don't develop a guilt complex.'

I could sense that Bernie was not his most charming and diplomatic self today. I suppose that when the market is surging ahead, as it seemed to be doing at the moment, stockbrokers felt the pressure, just like other people. All the same, I had invested half a million quid in a portfolio of blue chips and was entitled to his advice.

'How's ICI?' I asked.

'Oh, not bad. They've put on a couple of pence since you bought them. Not enough to cover the commission yet but heading in the right direction. Must go now, old boy. Another client on the line.'

I sat back and reviewed my portfolio. I know that some folks, lounging on their yachts in the Mediterranean, have what are known as discretionary accounts. They just hand over the money and tell their broker to get on with it. I liked to feel the cash flowing through my fingers. And I hadn't done too badly for a novice. I owned part of ICI, British Petroleum, Courtaulds, Marks and Spencer, Ecclesiastical Properties and oily options (or was it the other way about? I wouldn't know until I got the contract note). The one share I wasn't terribly happy about was Euro Jaunts.

'I've never heard of anything so daft,' said Mrs S., flicking through several back numbers of the Daily Smut. 'Whoever wants to know where the butter mountains are?'

I was inclined to agree. I shouldn't have let Freddy twist my arm.

The Mail was full of the bull market the following morning. The leaders were roaring ahead, it said, under the impetus of lower interest rates and a strong pound. Even second and third rank stocks had been marked up in sympathy.

At five to nine, Freddy was on the blower, full of enthusiasm.

'The market's got the wind behind it,' he gasped. 'I advise you to strike while the iron's hot.'

'What, sell? I've only just bought.'

'Not sell, old boy. Buy! Join the gold rush!'

Mrs S. was glowering across the breakfast table.

'I don't think I can really afford any more at the moment,' I said. 'In fact, I've been having second thoughts about those Euro Jaunts.'

'Second thoughts?'

'Yes, I think I'll sell and just stick to the blue chips.'

Freddy sucked in a lungful of bracing, early-morning air.

'Might be difficult, might be difficult. Not much demand for them, I'm afraid.'

'But if they're such a good investment somebody will want them?'

'Not necessarily, old boy. The market's got bigger things on its mind just now.'

'They certainly don't seem to be in the same class as the other shares in my portfolio.'

'Not yet,' said Freddy. 'But who'd have thought five years ago that the Channel Tunnel would be up and running?'

He had a point.

'All right,' I said. 'I'll hang on to them for the time being. But, if you can find a buyer, I shan't be sorry to lose them.'

'Leave it with me, old boy. I'll see what I can do.'

5. The Irish connection

Is human nature incurably depraved? Interesting question, that. I found it on Page One of a book by Mr George Bernard Shaw. He was one of those Irishmen who came over on the ferry when the taties ran out. Soon made himself at home, all right. Joined the Labour Party and had dinner with Uncle Joe – in Moscow! I saw a picture of him once. Looked as if he could do with a good feed. Apparently, he didn't believe in an enterprise culture. Thought everybody ought to be equal. Fair shares for all, that sort of thing. If he'd had his way, the Stock Exchange would have been closed down, or at least nationalised. A right Commo, if you ask me. If anybody was depraved, it was him.

Personally, I reckon there's a streak of goodness in everybody, if you dig deep enough. Take Freddy, for example. Good old Freddy with the carnation in his buttonhole. Two months ago, I wouldn't have known the difference between a put option and a black hole. Now, thanks to Freddy, I could find my way around the City blindfold. He has taught me all I know. Bernie? I'm not so sure. Bit of a slippery customer, if you ask me (the type GBS had in mind when he was ranting and raving about the capitalist system). Do you know, I've paid him £12,638 in commission so far? And half the time he can't even be bothered to answer the telephone. Mind you, Freddy and his wine lakes make the old mind boggle occasionally.

'Anything in the Smut about Euromountains?' I asked Mrs S. as we perused the financial news.

'Not a sausage,' said Mrs S. 'If you ask me, you're flogging a dead horse.'

'That's the trouble. I can't flog 'em.'

You'd think with the market going up the way it was – 'Bull market rages on', The Times reported – ditching a few worthless shares would be as easy as falling off a log. But, no. Some shares are slow movers.

'I think I'll give Bernie a ring,' I said. 'Tell him to get rid of them at any price.'

'By the way, the phone bill came this morning,' said Mrs S. 'I've never known it so high.'

'Help yourself from under the mattress, love,' I said. 'You can't run a business without having to fork out occasionally.'

Bernie was being more slippery than usual this morning. His offsider, a nasally guy I had never met, kept saying he was with a client, on the phone, having a pee, anything to fob me off. When I was at last able to pin him down I was feeling like GBS – a bit hot under the collar.

'I thought you were my stockbroker?' I said, throwing the weight of my cheque books about.

'So I am, dear boy, so I am. But you must appreciate that we are in the grip of the most almighty bull market that we have seen for years. I can't drop everything to deal personally with every one of my clients, however much I would like to.'

'Perhaps you would be able to devote more time to your clients if you had fewer of them?' I said, pointedly.

'I don't quite follow, old boy?'

I could tell he was thinking fast. Probably worried about those little old pennies that kept rolling his way.

'What I mean is that, unless I get better service, I shall take my account elsewhere.'

'My dear chap!' exclaimed Bernie, full of apologies. 'I certainly didn't mean to imply that you were less valued than my other clients. In fact, let's not beat about the bush, you are the most important – and valuable – client I have. Now, what can I do for you?'

'First of all,' I said, determined not to be taken in by flannel, 'you can tell me what's happened to Euro Jaunts.'

'Ah, well, I regret to say that you are still the owner of fifty thousand of them. I think Freddy did try to explain that there's not much demand for them at the moment.'

'Not even in the midst of the most almighty bull market for years?'

'If you recall,' said Bernie, 'you bought them for long-term investment, with your eye on 1992 and all that.'

'I bought them because I had my arm twisted,' I said. 'I'm selling on instinct. So please get rid of them.'

'Will do, old boy. At best?'

Something about his 'old boy' attitude got right up my nose. As I said earlier, he wasn't like Freddy, who had a streak of goodness in him, even if it was not always visible. Bernie was an out-and-out capitalist, the sort of person who would vote Conservative. I lost my temper – something I haven't done since I came into money.

'Yes, even better than best, old boy,' I snapped. 'And while you're at it, you can sell the rest of my shares as well.'

'Sell? Everything?' asked Bernie.

'Yes. Everything. Sell, sell, sell!'

'You realise that, by selling now, you could lose a fortune?' said Bernie, remaining calm, despite my anger. 'This market is set to continue for months yet.'

'I don't care,' I said. 'Sell!'

And I slammed down the phone.

Mrs S. had already put the kettle on to make a cup of coffee. I wondered if it was all this caffeine I was drinking that was making me irritable.

'Well, your bank managers should be pleased,' said Mrs S.

'Yes. About time I earned some interest instead of keeping my stockbroker.'

We tuned into LBC while drinking the coffee. The market was still going up. I wondered if I had done the right thing. Investment decisions should be taken with a cool head, not on the spur of the moment, in a filthy temper. But if other people could get through to their broker, as they obviously could, I reckoned I should be able to contact mine without making Mrs S. get out her worry beads everytime she thought of the phone bill.

'What you need is a change of scene,' she said. 'Something to take your mind off the market. Do you realise you haven't had a holiday, even though you've got all that money?'

'How can I go on holiday when I'm up to my neck in risk?' I snapped.

'All right, there's no need to bite my head off. I was only thinking of your welfare.'

'I'm sorry, Mrs S.,' I said. 'I didn't mean it. You know that.

Why don't we take a day trip to France and stock up with duty-free?'

'Why bother with duty-free when you've got enough money to buy a whole vineyard?' asked Mrs S., displaying a logic not normally associated with her sex.

'You're right,' I said. 'Why don't we just buy a vineyard?'

'Because you don't know how to make wine,' replied Mrs S., with the same devastating logic.

'We could hire somebody to do it.'

'Why do you think the Frogs . . .' – I was surprised to hear her refer to our neighbours across the Channel in such crude terms; I expect she had picked it up by reading the Daily Smut – 'Why do you think the Frogs are selling their vineyards? Because of all that wine in the lake.'

Something clicked at the back of my mind. Perhaps these new-fangled Euromaps of Freddy's weren't such a bad idea, after all.

'We'll just go for the ride, then, and have a look at the countryside.'

The boat train was crowded. Hundreds of kids, and their parents, all going to see what makes the Froggies hop. Fortunately, there were no soccer hooligans although some of the kids looked as if they might develop that way.

'No discipline, that's the trouble,' said Mrs S. 'If they were my kids, I'd give 'em a clip round the ear.'

I had never thought of Mrs S. as a mother before. I didn't like to ask whether she had any kids and was therefore speaking from experience. Better to let sleeping dogs lie, especially as Mr S. had run off with the bird.

Admittedly, travelling first class, we didn't have to mix with the hoi polloi more than necessary. At Folkestone, however, came a bit of a shock. The boat was only one class. Poor Mrs S. was suffering in silence.

'It'll be better when they build the tunnel,' I said. 'Then we can go first class all the way.'

'When they build the tunnel,' said Mrs S., meaningfully. She was still getting over the disappointment of not finding a large hole as Ashford.

They say that a change is as good as a rest and there's nothing like a sea breeze for blowing away the cares of the Stock Exchange. We were almost at Calais before a nagging doubt surfaced.

'I wonder what the market's doing?' I said.

'Doesn't matter, does it?' said Mrs S. 'You're out of it.'

'Still like to keep abreast,' I said. 'Maybe I was a bit too quick on the draw. I guess Bernie was only doing his best.'

'Yes – but who for?'

Mrs S. told me what her old grandfather always used to say about Calais and it was clear that times had changed. If this was Calais, I thought, I'll go to Southall next time. You'd think the British hadn't got any supermarkets at home. They even had the English papers there. I picked up the Evening Standard at the hypermarche.

'Market takes a breather' ran the story on the City page. 'Share prices looked distinctly toppy today as dealers wondered if the bull market had run out of steam.'

'I thought we had come here to get away from all that?' asked Mrs S., with a touch of pique.

'Just looking,' I said. 'No harm in keeping abreast of the news.'

'That's the trouble with shares,' she replied. 'You get hooked, if you're not careful.'

'Not me,' I said. 'I'm no junkie. Come on, let's go and find somewhere to eat.'

'Not too far,' pleaded Mrs S. 'We don't want to miss the boat.'

'What's the hurry?' I asked. 'We don't have to get back tonight. We can stay here, if necessary.'

'But I didn't bring my nightie!' cried Mrs S.

'This is France – remember? You can sleep in your birthday suit, if you like.'

Mrs S. shot me a look of terror.

'Nobody will see you,' I said, trying to reassure her, 'unless you ask for a cup of tea in bed.'

The spasm passed and the light in her eyes dimmed.

We walked along the quai for a while, then down the back

streets of the old town. I could have done with one of Freddy's maps. One or two restaurants; nothing very special, though. Then we came across a little bistro, La Republique. It looked intimate and romantic and the food smelled good. Most importantly, there seemed to be no British there.

'Would you be wanting lunch, then?' the waiter asked, his Irish brogue breaking the spell and transporting us straight back to Kilburn.

'That was the general idea,' I said.

Paddy brought the menu. I could see he was dying to know whether we were just day trippers or had come on more important business. I was dying to know what an Irishman was doing in the back streets of Calais. But, when you're a millionaire, you don't strike up casual conversations with waiters. I ordered and let him guess why we were on the wrong side of the Channel. Mrs S. was studying our fellow diners.

'This is a pretty rum joint you've brought me to,' she said, none too softly. 'I've never seen such a bunch of crooks in all my life.'

'They're not crooks, just foreigners,' I explained. 'They all look like that.'

I couldn't help comparing the place with the Trattoria del Duce in Brighton. I must say, the food at Brighton looked a lot fresher, as though the environmental health officer had visited the premises occasionally. Here, in Calais, it had more of an oily look about it. Nice, though; I'm not complaining. Pretty reasonable, too. Fifty francs for a three-course meal. Our Irish friend brought the bill on a saucer, Continental style.

'Enjoy your lunch, then?' he asked.

'Not bad,' I said. 'Better than McDonalds.'

He frowned slightly. Maybe he had a friend in McDonalds who made the chips. Very loyal to their friends, the Irish.

'Tell me,' I said, curiosity getting the better of me, 'what's a fellah like you doing in a place like this? Don't they pay you enough at home?'

'Tis not a question of pay,' he said. 'More of serving the community.'

I didn't know if the guy was trying to be funny or not. The

Irish have a funny sense of humour, as anyone who has ever seen Wogan would appreciate. Maybe he was attached to some religious order and atoned for his sins by eating frog food every day. I pulled out my cheque book.

'You'll take a cheque?'

'Sure.'

The cheque was drawn on my Italian bank, the Banco di Roma. Most of my other accounts had been plundered to pay for my dealings on the Stock Exchange. I thought an Italian bank would impress the frogs. But Paddy didn't bat an eyelid.

'My lira account,' I joked.

'Lira?'

'L.I.R.A. But I'll pay in francs, if you like.'

'Lire will do.'

He took the cheque and the guarantee card to the desk and had a quick word with le patron. Unless I am mistaken, the little Frenchy gave me a good, hard look. I hoped he didn't think I was in the same class as the rest of his shifty-looking customers. Then Paddy brought the receipt.

'If you're looking for somewhere to stay,' he said, 'try this.'

And he slipped me a card for L'hotel du Logh.

'Thanks,' I said. 'We were wondering whether to stay the night.'

'I think you'll find everything you need there.'

God knows how long we had sat in the bistro eating our lunch – or what passes for lunch in Froggy land when you're not pushed for time – but it was almost dark when we came out.

'We'll never make the boat now,' said Mrs S.

'What's the hurry?' I asked. 'We'll stay overnight. Book into the hotel and, when we've recovered, go to a night club. How would that suit you?'

'I'm game for anything,' said Mrs S.

We stood on the pavement, looking for a taxi. Lesson Number One: they drive on the wrong side of the road in France. Lesson Number Two: if you want a taxi in Calais, don't look like an English tourist. And, if you do look like an English tourist, have a few choice words handy when the buggers don't stop. We were on the point of walking down to the harbour and getting the night ferry home when Mrs S. pointed out that we were standing outside the Hotel du Logh.

'Why the hell didn't he say it was just round the corner?' I demanded.

'Perhaps he thought we knew.'

We marched up to the desk and for the first time I wondered how I would get on with the language of the frogs. I never got past irregular verbs at school. This guy who looked as though he might own the joint was sitting there, reading the paper.

'Excusez-moi, monsieur,' I said. 'Parlez vous anglais?'

'Of course, monsieur. Everybody in Calais speaks English. You would like a room for the night?'

'Two rooms, actually,' I said hurriedly, lest he get the wrong idea.

'I'm sorry, monsieur. We have one single and one double, which I can let you have for the price of a single, if you like.'

Well, even a millionaire doesn't turn down the chance of getting three for the price of two. A fifty per cent reduction, unless I'm mistaken.

'We'll take them,' I said.

'Just for one night, monsieur?'

'Yeah. We're going home in the morning.'

'That reminds me, I didn't put the milk bottles out,' said Mrs S.

'You have no luggage, monsieur?'

'We're travelling light,' I said.

He looked very thoughtful. I wondered if he was going to offer me some pyjamas.

Instead, he said: 'The rooms are two hundred and fifty francs, monsieur. It is the custom in this hotel to pay for them in advance.'

So that was it! Trust the frogs to put the health of their bank accounts before the welfare of their clients! But it was fair enough, I suppose. After all, we had just blown in off the street; we could easily have cut and run – although Mrs S. might have been reluctant to stir at daybreak without her nightie. I took out the cheque book so recently used to pay our way at the bistro. Then I remembered that Mrs S. had another book, issued by my South American bank, in her bag. ('For emergencies,' she said.) As the Banco di Roma had gone down like a lead balloon with Paddy at the bistro, I thought I would polish my jet-set image with the Bank of La Paz.

The guy looked at it with the merest flicker of interest and locked it in the safe.

'Thank you, monsieur,' was all he said.

Dead loss, really, trying to impress foreigners with foreign banks. Maybe I should have stuck to Barclaycard.

We followed him up the stairs – the Hotel du Logh was built before lifts were invented – and along a corridor. It smelled a bit musty, if you ask me. Or maybe somebody had been smoking one of those Turkish cigarettes.

'Here you are,' he said, opening the door to Number Eleven, 'I will put madame in here, with the double bed, and you, monsieur, can take Number Ten next door. There is a connecting door,' he added, 'which may come in useful.'

He bowed, in the ever-so-polite manner that frogs have, and went downstairs again. Mrs S. hovered nervously at the door to her room. She seemed at a bit of a loss.

'Why don't we both put our feet up for a while?' I suggested. 'Stretch out and let the old tum relax?'

Mrs S. giggled and glanced at the double bed.

'Give me a shout when you're ready to go out,' I added. 'I'm only next door.'

If I were Charles Dickens or, say, Jeffrey Archer, I could probably describe the feeling of well-being that came over me as I kicked off my shoes. But when you're stuffed to the gills with escallopes de veal and pickled walnuts, marinated in half a litre of house wine, it's not so easy. Suffice it to say that, as I flopped down on the mattress, the lights of the ferry flickered in the harbour while, in the street below my window, the natives made their way homewards. In villas and apartments all over Calais, little women who had been slaving over a hot stove waited anxiously for their menfolk to return. In some houses, where liberté and egalité had been taken literally and the bloke stayed at home minding the kids, the little woman was down there, in the traffic jam, working herself up into a right Gallic temper.

Anyway, up here on the first floor of the Hotel du Logh, I fell into a trouble-free sleep.

I was awoken by a faint tapping at the inter-communicating door. The old head was a bit muzzy and in the darkness I couldn't think where I was. The tapping continued. I stumbled about (the flickering lights of the ferry in the harbour didn't reach this far) and felt for the lock. The door swung open to reveal Mrs S. all dressed up to the nines.

'I didn't think you had brought a change of clothes with you!' I gasped.

In the half light, she was looking a bit of all right and much younger than her years. (I could never figure out how old she was. As I said, she had let herself go a bit and you can't erase twenty years of wear and tear on a day trip to Calais.)

'I just nipped down to the shops to see what there was,' she explained. 'It's foreign. Do you like it?'

'Smashing!' I cried. 'You look just smashing! We'll have to go somewhere really special now.'

Mrs S. looked real pleased with the compliment. It was hard to tell with the light behind her but I think she blushed.

'I'll just add the finishing touches while you get ready,' she said.

In addition to the frock – a black affair, with splashes of red here and there – Mrs S. had obviously invested in a bottle of scent. Femme Fatale, she said it was called. Distant Early Warning, I would have said. At least it over-powered the Turkish fag smell.

'Madame and Monsieur are going out to dinner?' said our French friend with a blinding glimpse of the obvious.

'I suppose you don't know of a good night club where they don't charge the earth for a Coke?' I remarked.

'Coke?'

'Yes. We've had enough of alcohol for one day. We're on a different kick now, eh, Mrs S?'

Mrs S. squeezed my arm to confirm that we were.

Jacques said: 'You wait a minute. I will call a taxi and he will take you to the best night club in town.'

'It's not one of them discotheques, is it?' asked Mrs S.,

suspiciously.

'Oh, no, madame,' replied Jacques, deeply offended. 'You asked for a night club; I will address you to a night club. You will find all you want there.'

I'll say one thing for the frogs; if you've got the money, they don't mind who you are. None of this probing into your background to see if you're an Old Etonian. That's what comes from being a republic, I suppose. All their aristocrats were done in. When we arrived at the club, no-one even demanded to see our passports. We just handed over a few francs and they let us in.

The first thing that struck me was this strange smell, as though somebody was burning incense. It reminded me of the hotel, only here it was much stronger. Perhaps it was just l'odour naturelle. From what I'd heard, the frogs don't take a bath more than once in a blue moon. Just wash their feet every so often in one of these bidet things.

'Smells like they could do with a plumber,' observed Mrs S. as this bloke – I'm sure he was a fairy – showed us to our table.

'Don't worry,' I said. 'You're more than a match for anything the frogs can throw at us.'

The fairy hung about, obviously expecting us to place an order.

'What time does the floor show come on?' I asked.

'Floor show?'

'Yes. Cabaret. Birds, boobs, that sort of thing.'

'I'm sorry, sir. There is no cabaret here.'

'No cabaret?'

'No cabaret.'

'What about a band?' asked Mrs S. 'You must have a band?'

'Sometimes they play, sometimes they don't,' the fairy said, shrugging his shoulders. 'It depends how they feel.'

I looked at Mrs S. and she looked at me. To think that we had paid fifty francs, in cash, to get in this joint and all it was was a low-class dive with something wrong with the drains. The fairy could see we were annoyed.

'If you would like to place an order, I'll see what can be done,' he said.

I felt sorry for Mrs S., really. Here she was, all decked out like a pleasure streamer in full rig, and not even a two-piece combo going through a mime routine. I would have a word with Jacques when we returned to the hotel. I sensed that the fairy was waiting

'What are you going to have, Mrs S? A double brandy?'

'I feel like one,' she said. 'But I don't think we'll be stopping here long. I'll have an orange juice.'

'Orange juice and a Coke,' I said to the fairy, who pranced off into the gloom.

Now that my eyes were adjusting to the atmosphere, I had a decco at the other customers. Most of them seemed totally unaware of our presence. They sat at the small tables, staring vacantly at each other over the candles, or into space. Most of them were young although at one table I thought I recognised one of the shifty-looking customers from the bistro.

The fairy returned with two orange juices and a sachet of glucose or something. I didn't argue. Trying to explain the difference between Coke and orange juice at this time of night wasn't worth the effort. Mrs S. poked the sachet doubtfully.

'Saccarine, I suppose. But if it has come from the kitchen, I'm not having anything to do with it.'

'Tastes all right without it,' I said, sampling the juice. 'Tesco special, unless I'm mistaken.'

'We could have stayed at home for that,' said Mrs S. 'In fact, we could have amused ourselves at the hotel for a lot less than it cost to get in here.'

I had to admit that it was a bit of a dead loss.

'Wait till I get my hands on that bloody Jacques,' I said. 'He obviously hasn't a clue about what goes on in this town.'

The fairy came back and shrugged apologetically.

'I'm sorry, monsieur. The band is having a smoke at the moment. Maybe one hour; maybe two. You like another drink?'

'No, thank you,' I said. 'We're going. L'addition, s'il vous plait.'

'This way, monsieur.'

This time, we almost tripped over the bodies on the floor.

They had sort of lolled over until they fell off their chairs. And there wasn't all that much booze around, either.

'That will be seven hundred francs, monsieur,' the fairy said, adopting a very mercenary posture.

'Seven hundred francs? For a couple of drinks?'

The fairy shrugged again. The shifty-looking guy from the bistro was leaning against the door. I didn't like it.

'I'll have to give you a cheque, I'm afraid,' I said, swallowing hard.

'That's all right, monsieur.'

'How much is seven hundred francs?' I asked Mrs S. as I drew another cheque on the Bolivian account.

'I don't know, but it's a rip-off,' said Mrs S., not mincing her words.

'Thank you, monsieur,' the fairy said, showing the cheque quickly to the unsavoury gent by the door. 'I hope you had a good trip?'

'Oh, marvellous,' I said. 'Absolutely bloody wonderful. I must come here again, especially for the cabaret.'

As we were leaving, a little guy in a dark suit and white shoes – probably the band leader, I thought – came out of the office and ran after us. He was clutching a Teddy bear.

'Madame would like something to remember us by,' he said, by way of introduction.

'I wouldn't be too sure about that,' said Mrs S., eyeing him coldly.

Charming bugger, I thought. They're all the same, these foreigners. Take your money, then try to make up for it with a bit of the old flannel and garlic.

'Perhaps, as a gesture of our appreciation, you would care to accept this little gift?' he said, thrusting Teddy into her arms.

Mrs S. softened. I could feel the tension ease, even in the half light.

'That's very kind of you,' she said.

'Not at all, madame. How do you say – the boot is on the other foot?'

For seven hundred francs, he was dead right. But Mrs S. seemed quite taken with her furry friend so I let the matter drop.

The wop – he was either Spanish or Italian – smiled ingratiatingly and bade us goodnight.

'What do we do now?' I asked, searching for the lights of the ferry flickering in the harbour, etc., but finding only the side lights of a taxi, waiting for hire.

'Let's go and have something to eat,' said Mrs S.

Well, to cut a long story short, we ended up at a fish restaurant down on the quai, knocking back turbot and chips, plus a bottle of champagne, just to make up for the disappointment of the club. By the time we had got through the champers Mrs S. was a changed woman. The lights were better here, too. We could see the other diners and they could see us. Mrs S. turned one or two heads, I can tell you. Fortunately, the Femme Fatale had lost some of its strength by now, what with the salt air and the fried fish. All the same, she was still pretty fragrant by the time we came to go.

'Sure you wouldn't like one for the road?' I asked as the patron arrived with the bill.

Mrs S. giggled. She was more like her old self.

'Oh, all right, then. Just a small one. For Teddy.'

Well, as I said, France is the place to get the old plonk in your veins and by the time we arrived back at the hotel I could just about see the cobblestones in front of me. Once I had to relieve myself in the gutter.

'Hooligan!' giggled Mrs S., pretending to look the other way.

'Drunken English on the rampage!' I retorted.

The concierge, Jacques, was nowhere to be seen. Locked himself up for his own protection, I suppose. Must have known I'd give him an earful when I saw him again. Seven hundred francs for a couple of orange drinks and a Teddy bear! Just as well I was a millionaire. We staggered up the stairs, holding on to each other for support, and along the corridor to room Number Eleven. Mrs S. fumbled for her key and unlocked the door. We both fell inside. All I saw was the double bed, its covers back and looking very inviting.

That's all I remember until about half past ten the following morning when I woke up, fully dressed and a bit stiff. There was no sign of Mrs S., thank God. But here was I, in her bed. Or, rather, on her bed. What was I doing here? I splashed my face with cold water and tried to recall what had happened. Had anything happened? I hoped to God that it had not. But, as I have noted before, Mrs S. is a fine-looking woman and what with the Femme Fatale and the alcohol . . .

I tapped gently on the communicating door. I tried the handle. It was unlocked. I tapped again and cautiously opened it. Mrs S. was there, reading the Daily Smut.

'Good morning,' I said. 'I must have slept in your bed.'

'Slept is the word,' she said, casting me a withering look.

'I'm very sorry,' I said. 'I hope you were able to get a bit of shut-eye?'

'Teddy and I spent a very enjoyable night in a single bed, together,' she replied. 'I suggest you have a shower and we'll catch the boat.'

To say that relations were a bit strained as we made our way to the docks in a taxi was putting it mildly. Mrs S. had on one of her landlady moods. I noticed that she kept glancing at herself in the mirror, as though to check on her looks.

'You're looking very well this morning,' I said gallantly, but the remark fell on stony ground.

For some reason, I was being given the old cold shoulder.

However, it was not a time for philosophical reflection. We were travelling home with what appeared to be a bunch of apprentice Borstal boys and their minders. The thought of what they might do when the bar opened and we were beyond reach of the coast guards made Mrs S. snap out of herself.

'Why couldn't they leave 'em in France?' she demanded. 'The French have capital punishment, don't they?'

'I'm not sure,' I replied. 'I know they closed down Devil's Island.'

'More's the pity,' grumbled Mrs S.

Strangely enough, it was not the Borstal boys who made their presence felt as we headed out to sea. They were on their best behaviour, obviously hoping for parole. It was the screaming kids from Miss Nancy's Kindergarten who began to get on the nerves. I mean, what can you do with a snotty five-year-old who throws a tantrum in mid-Channel?

'Why doesn't somebody do something?' asked Mrs S., getting a bit edgy again.

I quite agreed. Miss Nancy – or whoever it was in charge of the little darlings – was completely out of her depth. She simply turned a blind eye, or a deaf ear, as her charges ran amok.

'Maybe she had been told to drown them but chickened out,' I said, as the star pupil – a mini-skirted monster with a piercing scream – continued to demand attention.

'Oh, for goodness sake!' cried Mrs S., jumping to her feet and advancing on the screaming child. 'Here! Take Teddy and be kind to him! He doesn't like a lot of noise.'

She stumped back to her deck chair, oblivious to the grateful glances of other passengers, and brushed herself down. Teddy had apparently been stuffed with a cheap, white powder, not cuddly cotton wool.

The child stopped screaming. Miss Nancy looked on in her serene way. The other children gathered round to examine the new toy.

'I didn't really want a Teddy bear, anyway,' said Mrs S., with a touch of bravado. 'Only little girls have those when they've nothing better to cuddle in bed.'

I was about to remind her that Teddy had spent the night between her very own sheets but, on second thoughts, decided to let the matter drop. No point in opening old wounds.

That just about wraps up our trip to France, really. Frankly, I couldn't see much scope for Freddy's little maps. When we got off at Dover, we walked straight through Customs with our whisky and gin and boarded the London train. The only person who seemed the least bit interested was this foreign gent, lounging near the ticket barrier. He seemed about to come up to us, then changed his mind and walked away. Miss Nancy and her kids were a long way behind, thank God. I hoped the train would pull out before they reached the platform. The thought of travelling with them all the way to Victoria was more than a millionaire could bear.

Was it the guard's whistle or the shriek of a spoiled brat? From our carriage it was hard to tell. But down in the Customs

Hall there seemed to be some sort of commotion. Whatever it was, we would never know. The train began to move.

'I told you I hadn't put out the milk bottles,' said Mrs S., as we arrived home. 'Now I'll have to nip down to the shops or we won't have any for breakfast.'

'Don't worry about milk,' I said, dumping the duty free on the table. 'We'll have one of these. It's what big girls drink.'

I got a bottle of tonic water from the fridge.

'Sorry about last night,' I said. 'You'd think the frogs would know what cabaret meant.'

'Not your fault,' she said generously. 'Next time we'll know better.'

'Let's see what's on the news,' I said, switching on the telly. 'Catch up with what's happened while we've been away.'

The picture came into focus. The guy with red hair who sat on a lesbian was speaking.

'And now to end the news here are the main points again,' he said. 'On the London Stock Exchange, share prices have suffered their biggest one-day fall for eight months. At the close, the F.T. index was down nearly eighty points. And at Dover, police and Customs officials believe they have smashed an IRA drugs ring that used a kindergarten to smuggle cocaine into Britain. A Bolivian with an Irish passport has been arrested and is expected to be charged with attempted kidnapping.'

'Probably that bloke we saw hanging around the docks,' I said, taking a swig of G&T.

'Probably,' said Mrs S. 'Sshh! I want to hear the weather forecast.'

6. *Prerogatives of the rich*

Freddy was on the doorstep bright and early the following morning. He had never been to the house before and his presence obviously signalled some sort of crisis. Mrs S. showed him into the kitchen where I was having breakfast.

'Congratulations, old boy!' he said, shaking my hand and taking a seat on the far side of the marmalade. 'A magnificent piece of timing.'

'Timing? What timing?'

'Why, selling out before the market collapsed. Tell me, did you get wind of it somewhere?'

To be perfectly honest, I couldn't remember why I had lost my temper and told Bernie to sell.

'I certainly wasn't happy about the way things were going,' I said, ambiguously.

'Bernie was most impressed,' said Freddy. 'Timing is everything in the market. The art of investment is not so much what, but when.'

'Buy cheap and sell dear,' I said. 'You can't go wrong.'

'Quite,' said Freddy. 'But most people are so blinded by greed that they cannot bring themselves to sell.'

'It's a bit like horse racing,' I said. 'You've gotta quit while you're winning. Any chance of another cup of tea, Mrs S?'

Freddy pulled his moustache and looked a bit uncomfortable.

'Of course, Bernie is very upset that he has apparently lost you as a client,' he said. 'I think you'll agree that, as brokers go, he's probably no worse than average. After all, he did help you to make a quick killing on Northern Puds.'

'Yeah, well, perhaps he's not so bad, then,' I conceded, stirring the tea. 'It's just that I reckon a client ought to be able to reach his broker now and again – or what's the point of having one? You might just as well programme yourself into a computer.'

'I quite agree,' said Freddy. 'What you need is the personal touch. Why not give him a ring? I'm sure he would be delighted to hear from you.'

'I've no doubt he would,' said I. 'I see from my contract notes that he has already earned about twenty thousand quid in commission.'

'That's true, old boy,' said Freddy, with a winning smile. 'But look how much you've made.'

I couldn't argue with that. I guessed I must have made a small fortune on ICI, Marks and British Petroleum. Not to mention the initial windfall in Northern Puds.

'What's happening about Euro Jaunts?' I asked, suddenly remembering the lame duck of my portfolio.

'Ah, well, I'm glad you asked about that,' said Freddy. 'I'm afraid that's one of life's little losers. You said sell, so we sold.'

'How much?' asked Mrs S., suddenly taking an interest.

'I reckon you've blown about twenty grand, plus commission, of course.'

'I suppose that more or less cancels out my gain on Marks and ICI?'

'I wouldn't say that, old boy. We'll have to wait and see how much Bernie was able to get. But I should think you're on the winning side.'

On the winning side! After getting out on the top floor with the real smart guys! I ought to have been streets ahead.

'I think I'll give the market a miss for a while,' I said. 'I can't see much point in buying shares if I'm going to lose money all the time.'

'But don't you see? Now's the time to buy. While they're cheap.'

'Not what; when?'

'Exactly.'

They say that nobody rings a bell when the market hits the top or the bottom. You just have to watch for the signs. I wondered if it was an omen that Freddy had rung the bell on the front door.

'What's the market doing this morning?' I asked.

'Oh, sort of consolidating,' said Freddy, vaguely.

'What does that mean?' demanded Mrs S.

'It means that the panic is over,' said Freddy. 'A time for rational decisions again.'

'What do you recommend?' I asked, feeling myself being sucked into the mire.

'I don't think you'll go far wrong with a thousand of anything again,' said Freddy. 'Why not sink half a million or so in half a dozen high-yielding blue chips? That will at least provide a cushion if the market continues to slide.'

'I'd sooner have the money,' I said.

'That's the nature of the business, I'm afraid, old boy. We're talking about risk capital. Even your money in the bank is not entirely safe.'

Mrs S. looked up anxiously.

'Suppose the bank goes bust,' said Freddy. 'Some of these foreign outfits are a bit dodgy at the best of times. You've only got to have a rumour that they're run by the Mafia and – bingo! Kaput!'

Freddy certainly had a valid point. What was that Eye-tie outfit called – the one with the archbishopric as managing director? Ambrosia. I thought they made rice puddings. But this little wop fellah who was supposed to check the balance sheet every night was found dangling from a rope under Blackfriars Bridge. I remember that because I used to walk across the bridge every day on the way to work. Pockets weighed down with gold bricks, they say.

'Do you think I ought to move some of my funds out of the bank, then?' I asked.

'Well, I wouldn't say that any one bank was worse than the others,' said Freddy, looking happier now that Mrs S. had at last poured him a cup of tea. 'But the whole point of investment is to spread the risk.'

'Maybe I should buy some unit trusts,' I said. 'Don't they spread the risks?'

Freddy looked dubious.

'You don't want to get mixed up with those,' he said. 'They're mainly for the small investor. You can afford something better. And besides, unit trusts are not in it for love, you know. They make a pretty hefty charge for their services.'

'More than Bernie?' I asked.

Freddy shifted uncomfortably again.

'At least commissions are negotiable,' he said. 'Unit trust charges are fixed. And, don't forget, Bernie and I are always willing to give you advice.'

'Your advice has just cost me twenty thousand quid,' I said.

'Well, I'm sure if you have a word with Bernie, he'll reduce the commission on Euro Jaunts. Unfortunate error. I'm sure they would have come good in the long run.'

'In the long run,' I said, quoting the great economist, John Bassett Canes, 'we are all dead.'

'True, true,' said Freddy. 'We are all of us only mortal.'

By the time I had finished breakfast, it was coming up to eleven o'clock.

'Switch on the wireless and let's see what the market is doing,' I said to Mrs S.

The market was going up. That is to say, it had stopped going down. According to LBC, the bears were having to cover their positions.

'You'd think they'd look in the mirror before going to work,' said Mrs S.

'No, what they mean is that speculators short of stock are having to buy in before they lose money,' explained Freddy.

I could see that Mrs S. was now much wiser.

'Why would they be short of stock?' she asked. 'Isn't there enough to go round?'

'It means, dear lady, that they sold stock they didn't own. Now they are having to buy it – and they would prefer to buy it now, rather than tomorrow, when the price might be higher.'

'If the price is going up, does that mean we ought to buy some as well?' I asked.

'Of course, dear boy. That is what I have been trying to say. You ought to get a few shares under your belt before the market takes off again. Why not give Bernie a ring?'

Despite a feeling – also under my belt – that the bank was probably the safest haven during the current squall, I gave Bernie a quick tinkle after lunch.

'Delighted to have you back as a client, old boy,' he trilled, 'and I hope there won't be any further misunderstandings. The customer always comes first, eh?'

'If you want his custom,' I said. 'What's new?'

'Well,' said Bernie, 'I did hear a rumour that the Republic of Bongo was about to settle its debts. There's a fair bit of loan stock floating about; pretty cheap, too. You could pick up a bundle and make a killing.'

'Where is Bongo?' I asked.

'Oh, you know, one of those African countries. Borrowed to the hilt ten or fifteen yeas ago to build a hydro-electric scheme. Then somebody discovered they had no rivers and not much use for electricity, anyway. Of course, they defaulted on the loan as soon as they had it. The World Bank has been keeping them afloat till the cocoa crop dries.'

'Doesn't sound a very safe bet to me,' I said.

'You took the words right out of my mouth,' said Bernie. 'It is a bet, no doubt about it. A pure gamble. But,' he added, with the foresight one expects of a financial adviser, 'if they want to borrow more – which they do – they'll have to settle the outstanding loan.'

'How will they do that if they haven't got any money?'

'Easy, old boy. They come to some arrangement with the bank. You know, an interest-free bridging loan, that sort of thing. Maybe they can even get an advance on the cocoa crop. Then they can pay off their old debts and start all over again, defaulting on the new one.'

'And how would I make money out of that?' I asked.

'Well, if you had, say, a million quid's worth – nominal of course – they would have to cough up before they got any fresh money. You've got 'em by the short and curlies, so to speak.'

'Sounds to me as though they've got investors by the short and curlies,' I said.

Mrs S. gave me one of her old-fashioned looks – the one that registered disapproval of coarse language in her parlour.

'They have. But that's the first principle of finance, of course. Never give a sucker a break, especially if he's your bank manager.'

Those were my sentiments, too, and while I'm not one to

bear grudges the thought of having a fling at the expense of the pin-striped gits who preferred to lend to the Third World rather than to needy citizens at home had a certain appeal.

'I can't afford a million quid's worth,' I said. 'Not after Euro Jaunts.'

'They won't cost you anything near a million,' said Bernie. 'About ten per cent, at the most, I'd say.'

'I don't follow.'

'Put it this way: for every hundred quid's worth of stock you buy, it will cost you a tenner. Then, if the little black fellahs settle at fifty per cent, you've made four hundred per cent profit. Do you follow now?'

'It sounds a lot to me,' I said. 'Four hundred per cent?'

'Risk-reward ratio,' said Bernie. 'You can't expect people to venture into darkest Africa without getting something back. Tell you what,' he added, 'I'll see if I can pick up half a million quid's worth and we'll see how they run. That won't break the bank, eh?'

'Whose bank?' I asked.

'Yours,' said Bernie. 'Must go now, old boy. Don't want to miss the tide.'

As it was a nice day, we decided to visit the Jewish cemetery and see how the monumental masons were getting on with Mrs Rosenbaum's tombstone. Signor Scarlatti, the little Italian guy who was supposed to be doing the chiselling, had obviously caught the British disease. There was no sign of him – or the tombstone. Mrs S. was not unduly worried. We had written out the words on a sheet of A4 so there could be no mistake and even paid for the whole lot in advance.

'I expect he's got a lot to do, what with the oil well and all that,' said Mrs S. charitably.

I had forgotten the oil well. In fact, I do not recall seeing the name of Phoenix Hydrocarbons on the list of shares that Bernie was supposed to have sold before the crash.

'That's because you only bought options,' explained Mrs S.

'Did I? I don't remember.'

I phoned Bernie as soon as we got home.

'That's right, old boy,' he confirmed. 'Call options on the oil, puts on the property. What goes down might not come up. Might as well hold on till we know the worst. No point in throwing money down the drain.'

You're right there, I thought. Indeed, I could have poured my entire fortune down the sink of human misery, had I been so inclined. Every day since news of my win became public knowledge, the Post Office had delivered a whole stack of begging letters and hard luck stories. One bloke in Surrey reckoned that all he had left, after fighting for his country in two world wars, was a five-bedroomed house and a small, private income.

Actually, the blokes from the pools company come round every so often to make sure that we capitalists are not taken for a ride by standard-rate taxpayers. Some folks with a lot of dough they want to hang on to get real upset when some old woman from Finchley writes and says she is down to her last crust. That's why the pools people say, don't read 'em. Just chuck 'em away, unopened. If you like, they'll even take them to the tip. But how do you know what a letter says until you've read it? Besides, they're not all from old women in Finchley. Some are from young birds who have hit a bad patch very early in life.

'What's that you're reading?' asked Mrs S., as I weighed up the pros and cons of a letter from one Cheryl Braithwaite of Huddersfield.

'Oh, just another begging letter,' I said, casually putting it in my pocket, along with a photograph that Cheryl had kindly sent of herself.

Apparently, she was an orphan who had been brought up in a workhouse, where she toiled away from dawn till dusk (and even longer in winter) without the benefit of tender, loving care. Not only had she to work her fingers to the bone but she had been half starved and never been away on holiday. She just wanted somebody who could give her a leg up in the world.

Upstairs, in the safety of my room, I took the photograph of poor little Cheryl out of the envelope and stared at it for a while. Of course, what passed for malnutrition in Victorian times, when values were different, was not the same as what we called under-nourishment today. It was not just a question of getting enough oats (although, by the looks of her, she was getting enough of those). No, it was all to do with protein. Give a bird enough protein, I read somewhere, and she'll put on weight in all the right places.

Well, of all the begging letters I had received, this was the one that most touched my heart. Can't always just think of Number One, Sid, old son. Remember, you voted Labour last time and they believe in the redistribution of wealth. So I dashed off a quick letter to Miss Braithwaite, enclosing a fifty-pound note and suggesting that, if she would like a holiday, to give me a buzz. On second thoughts, that would not be such a good idea with Mrs S. listening to every word. No, poor under-nourished Cheryl could write to me, care of the Post Office, and tell me her plans.

One thing I have learned during my career is that you can't pull the wool over the eyes of your landlady. Mrs S. was suspicious, all right, but I knew she couldn't fathom out why. Women seem to have a sixth sense, you know, especially where other women are concerned; not, of course, that any woman was concerned – yet. But it was a long couple of days before I was able to call in at the Post Office and ask – not too guiltily, I hoped – if there was any mail for me.

'Blimey, Sid! Don't you get enough through the front door without having to pick up scented envelopes at the Post Office?' asked Harry, the sub-postmaster.

'Some letters get personal attention, some don't,' I said huffily.

Harry winked.

'I see,' he said. 'No good me writing to you about my misfortunes, then?'

''Fraid not.'

I took the envelope into the park before opening it. The scent was over-powering; worse than Femme Fatale. Funny how orphaned waifs can afford perfume, I thought. But never mind. She had taken the bait.

Dear Sid (she wrote),
    Thank you ever so much for the £50. I put it straight in the

drawer where I keep my underwear. It is between my panties and my suspender belt, waiting for a rainy day. You have no idea what joy you have brought into the life of a simple country girl. I would very much like to have a holiday in London and for you to show me around the City. I have heard so much about it. But if London is not convenient I have always had a hankering for Jersey, where one (or perhaps two!) can get lost in a crowd, especially at this time of year. Would you like to take me to Jersey? I'm sure we could both have a good time. If you could help me get away from this place and restore my health, I would be *very* grateful. Thank you for all your help so far.

Love,
Cheryl

P.S. Photo appreciated.

P.P.S. If you would like me to meet you in Jersey, please send £100 for the air fare.

Well, Sid, boy, you're on to a good thing here, I thought. You've struck a rich vein of human misery. Can't go wrong for a hundred quid, or £150 if you count the money already sent. And even if it costs a couple of hundred quid to get there and back myself, what of it? You can afford it. And why shouldn't I give a poor orphan girl a good time? Besides, Jersey was one of those places that I wanted to see. I hear they have a lot of millionaires there, so I would be mixing with people of my own class. It's also the place where you can open a bank account and not have snoopers from the Inland Revenue poking their noses into it every hour of the day. That's what I would tell Mrs S. I would need some excuse for going there. Investigating offshore banking facilities, I'd say. Best done in secrecy.

I slipped a cheque for £100 into an envelope and posted it first class to Huddersfield, with a note suggesting that she get the plane on Monday and I'd meet her at the airport. I'd recognise her, all right, from the photo. If there were any problems, I said, just drop a line by return and we'd do our best to sort them out.

Mrs S. was mightily suspicious, especially when I told her that I was going on a business trip that was not only private but extremely boring. It was not, unfortunately, the sort of trip she would enjoy, otherwise I would take her along. She said nothing. What could she say, really? I was old enough to lead my own life.

Promiscuity is the prerogative of the rich. The phrase had stuck in my mind since I was a young lad wondering why those middle-aged blokes with a bald patch on their heads and pot bellies always seemed to be accompanied by the most glamorous birds. It wasn't their sex appeal that drew the birds, that's for sure. Now that I was one of these so-called wealthy types I was a bit surprised that more in the way of talent hadn't come my way. But here was this poor orphan from Huddersfield, ready to be grateful for providing her with the first holiday of her miserable life. How was I to exercise that prerogative about which I have just spoken? In other words, how was I going to convince this bird that, in order to make sure she was properly fed and watered, we ought to share the same room – and preferably the same bed? Wouldn't it look bad if, when I met her at the airport, I said, 'Oh, by the way, I've booked you in as Mrs Arbuthnot. You're sleeping with me tonight'? She might march back to the plane and go straight home again. On the other hand, anybody from Huddersfield wouldn't want to go back again so I could afford to chance my arm a bit there.

What, I asked myself, would a gentleman do if he were in my position? A gentleman would book two rooms, that's what he'd do, preferably with a connecting door like Mrs S. and I had in that froggy hotel. On Jersey, expense would be no obstacle.

Suddenly it struck me. Oh, God! So that's why Mrs S. was giving me the cold shoulder on the way to the boat! Surely not? At her age, too. I glanced at her out of the corner of my eye as we had afternoon tea. She was, it's true, a fine-looking woman.

And one with a certain experience of life. But . . . Sid, boy, I said to myself, you've got to get away and find a real bit of crumpet your own age before you succumb to a fate worse than death.

Mrs S. was extremely busy and a bit short-tempered when I

set out for Jersey on the Monday morning.

'I'll be back at the end of the week,' I said.

'Drop me a postcard, if you've got time.'

I don't know if you've ever been to Jersey but it's a funny little place, all covered in plastic. I thought it was a huge campsite but, according to the bloke who sat next to me on the plane, the plastic is used to make the potatoes grow faster. I didn't think potatoes grew at this time of the year but, apparently, they were getting ready for the next crop. They'll be wrapping up their cows in plastic next, I thought, like them cucumbers with the extra skin.

I don't mind telling you but I was a bit nervous as we came in to land; not because the plane was buffeted by a sudden gust from the Atlantic but because I was taking a giant step along the road of sexual adventure. I had taken the plunge and booked the Huddersfield waif into the Grand Hotel under an assumed name – Mrs Arbuthnot. I told her in a quick note on Friday night to make herself at home and that I would meet her there. For all I knew, she was waiting there now, spending what remained of her £100 on a small drink at the bar.

I asked the receptionist whether my wife had arrived yet.

'No, sir,' he said. 'Did she not travel with you?'

'No, I've been on business on the Continent and she was due to meet me here.'

'I'll let you know as soon as she arrives, sir.'

'Thank you.'

I looked at my watch. I suppose if you're coming from Huddersfield it takes a while for the fog to clear. I decided to have lunch and see what the afternoon brought. I can't say I enjoyed the meal; I was too nervous. Even millionaires suffer from nerves, you know, especially when they're meeting some bird for the first time. I drank more than I ought to have done. By the time I had staggered up to my room I could just about find the bed.

The telephone was ringing. I sat up and blinked. Where was I? In the splendour of the Grand Hotel, Jersey. The phone demanded that somebody answer it.

'Hullo?' I said, picking up the receiver.

'Your wife has arrived, sir.'

Gulp! Beads of nervous sweat. How would Sid, the philanderer, compare with Sid, the philanthropist?

'Will you show her up?'

'Of course, sir.'

Will you show her up? That was a fine way for a bloke to treat his wife, unless they had been married for a long time. Still, what the hell? The guy at the desk could think what he liked.

There was a tap at the door. A gentle tap, as befitted a poor orphan girl about to greet her benefactor. The heart beat faster.

'Come in,' I said.

The voice seemed strangely remote, as though it were not mine. I wondered how I would explain the double bed.

The door opened and this blonde with the 38 inch bust stepped shyly into the room.

'Hi, sweety!' she said, not sounding at all like a Huddersfield waif. 'I don't think they believed I was Mrs Arbuthnot – but we won't worry over details, will we?'

She advanced towards me and stood there, arms akimbo, as though waiting for something.

'Well, aren't you going to kiss me? I'm your wife, remember?'

'Did you have a good flight?' I asked, playing for time.

The hussy laughed. A harsh, sardonic laugh, I thought.

'Smoother than yours, by the look of you. Why didn't you take off the sick bag?'

I was taken aback by this unexpected, full-frontal assault. What had I done to deserve it?

'I don't understand,' I said, the old head reeling under the impact of two enormous boobs and half a bottle of Bergerac, the local wine.

'Don't you, honey?'

'I thought you were a poor girl from the workhouse.'

'More fool you.'

'I see.'

In fact, I didn't see. My mind was a blank.

'You don't think I'd come all this way to meet a jerk like you, do you?' the hussy said.

As she spoke, the door opened and the porter brought in her luggage. At least, I thought he was the porter. But something about him, possibly the pistol he pointed towards me, told me that he had nothing to do with the hotel.

'One squeak and you're a dead duck, darling,' said Cheryl, becoming extremely businesslike. 'Now, tell me, where do you keep your wallet?'

I opened my mouth but nothing came out. The voice had died, along with my passion. The orphaned waif struck me an almighty blow across the mouth.

'Give,' she said. 'We haven't got all day.'

The guy with the gun was already rummaging through my coat pocket. He pulled out a small purchase I had made at the chemist earlier.

'You won't be needing these, chum,' he said, throwing them on the bed. 'Where's the cash?'

'I haven't been to the bank yet,' I said, hoping to throw them off the scent.

'That was most ungenerous of you, Sid,' the hussy said. 'How are we going to live if you don't give us cash?'

She picked up my overnight bag and tipped the contents on to the bed. Several items of interest fell out, including a new electronic calculator I had bought to keep track of my investments.

'What's this?' she said, picking up a small, brown envelope that I had forgotten about. I had, in fact, slipped a bundle of fivers in there and was going to give it to the poor girl at the end of our holiday, if she had been good.

'You might as well take it. They were for you, anyway.'

'Gee, thanks, Sid! What about his credit cards?' she asked her accomplice.

'You gotta Diners Card?' the thug demanded.

'No. Just ordinary credit cards,' I confessed.

By this time, a thin trickle of blood had run down my chin and was dripping on to my suit. I did a quick calculation of how much the trip was likely to cost me.

'Just take what you want,' I said, 'but leave me alone.'

'Oh, we're going to do that, all right, Sid, old sweety,' the hussy revealed. 'But I'm afraid you will be on your own for some time.'

She jerked her head towards the chair that the hotel had provided for its guests.

'Sit!' she barked, sounding like that woman on television.

I did as I was told. The little guy with the revolver whipped the tie from my neck and, before I could undo the top button, tied my hands behind the chair. Then he took a handkerchief from the pile on the bed and stuffed it into my mouth. Another hanky held the gag in place. After making sure I couldn't escape, he put the gun away. The orphaned waif was already counting the loot.

'You're hardly worth coming all this way for, do you know that?' she asked, ungratefully. 'Five hundred bloody miles just for a couple of credit cards, a bunch of fivers and . . . how much you got there, Leo?'

'Ninety five in notes and some loose change.'

'Leave him the change. I guess he'll want something to remember us by.'

She turned and flaunted – that's the only word to describe the hussy's manner – flaunted her breasts in front of me. Her eyes narrowed. Mine didn't.

'You're not only a dirty old man, Sid,' she hissed, 'but an incredibly stupid one. I suppose you think that, because you're rich, you can screw anybody who takes your fancy. Well, there are some things in this world that money can't buy – and I'm one of them.'

I wish I could have replied, put her right about my humanitarian instincts. But what can you say with a couple of Mrs S.'s freshly-ironed hankies in your mouth?

The little guy packed everything, including my electronic calculator, neatly into the case he had brought with him while the hussy blew me a kiss.

'Nice meeting you, Sid, old fellah. They serve breakfast in bed here so we'll order you some. Sleep well.'

I shall not describe the torment and misery of that night on a Louis the Fourteenth chair on the island of Jersey. But I can tell you it was not made any more comfortable by the fact that I had consumed a large amount of liquid at lunch. Eventually I must have dosed off because I awoke to find the chambermaid in the room, bearing a tray. She smiled and put the tray on the bedside table.

'Would you like the morning paper, sir?' she asked politely.

Well, perhaps you grow hardened to these things when you're on room service. I mean, there must be times when even the most conspicuous cough or knock at the door fails to warn the happy couple that refreshment is on the way. And some people, I know, do indulge in some mighty funny practices when their marriage is getting a little stale. But I wouldn't mind betting that it's not often, even in Jersey where, of course, they are exposed to Continental influences, that a chambermaid finds a guest trussed up like a turkey and busting for a leak.

'For Christ's sake undo this gag and let me breathe!' I cried, but, of course, it came out like Swahili.

I tried body language. I fixed her with my eyes. They were wild and staring. I could see them in the mirror.

'Would you like me to untie you?' she asked, very quick on the uptake now that we had established an understanding.

I nodded vigorously.

She moved tentatively behind me and picked at the knot holding my gag. I spat out Mrs S.'s clean hankies. Persil not only washes whiter but it tastes different, too.

'Thank you,' I said. 'If you could just manage the hands.'

'Who left you like this, then?' the chambermaid asked, concern spreading over her simple features.

I was about to say 'My wife'. But, before I could think of an alternative lie, my hands were free and I had other matters to attend to. With one bound, I was out of the chair and heading for the loo.

'Would you like me to take your breakfast away and come back when you're feeling better?' the maid asked.

'No, don't bother. I'll be all right in a minute.'

The maid departed. They train them well at the Grand. Courteous to the end.

Very odd, you know, but I really fancied breakfast. Ever since dawn, I had been staring at the jumble of clothes on the bed, not to mention items of a personal nature. Now, at last, I could tidy up and relax. Life had to go on. I poured a cup of tea and wondered how to explain my predicament.

I was on the horns of a dilemma. If I reported the mugging – I was a right mug, all right – the police would ask a lot of embarrassing questions. What was I doing meeting a lady who wasn't my wife in Jersey, etcetera, etcetera. The hotel would be none too pleased, either, having cops all over the place, taking finger prints and what not. And suppose the gutter Press, the sort that camped outside the door at Fulham for the best part of a week until they went off to harrass another millionaire, what if they got hold of the story? I could see the headlines now: Pools winner mugged in holiday island sex romp. I would never be able to look Mrs S. in the face again. But was I failing in my public duty by keeping quiet? Might not some other poor bloke, seeking a well-earned break from his missus, fall into the same trap? Perhaps they had already. How had they coped with their public duty?

By the time I had finished breakfast, I had decided to keep quiet. Sid, I said, you are a moral coward and stupid to boot. But your experience has proved one thing; silence, as well as promiscuity, is the prerogative of the rich. I could afford the loss. I examined my cut lip in the mirror. Nothing to worry about there, I thought. In a couple of days, it would have healed up nicely.

As soon as the banks opened, I went to report the loss of my credit cards. Of course, they had been milked dry. But things could have been worse. At a small cafe in the town centre, I did a quick calculation on the back of an envelope. Loss of two credit cards, approx. £2,000. Bundle of fivers, £200. Introductory gratuity, £50. Fare to Jersey for orphaned waif, £100, ditto Sid, £150 (first class). Hotel, probably about £300. Total loss, £3,000. As experience goes, it was cheap at the price.

Nevertheless, I was a bit miffed when I recalled the unkind words of the hussy from Huddersfield. (The address she gave, by the way, was false. I had a private detective check it out. It turned out to be an accommodation address.) Anyway, what stung me was her remark that I was hardly worth the effort.

93

Blimey! Two and a half thousand quid for a day's work! She wouldn't get that on the Youth Training Scheme. I wondered what she did with the money. Perhaps she had a stockbroker to support.

7. The peseta in your pocket

'You're back early,' said Mrs S., opening the door and letting me struggle in with my luggage. 'Business go off okay?'

'So, so,' I said, non-committally. 'What's the market been doing while I've been away?'

'I've been too busy to follow it, I'm afraid,' said Mrs S., with a touch of self-satisfaction.

'Oh?'

'I've had the rabbi round here to discuss the grave. Nice little man. Goes by the name of Rosenbaum.'

'That's your mother's name,' I said.

'Yes. It seems there could be a priest in the family.'

'Rabbi, you mean.'

'Priest, rabbi, archbishop. What does it matter, my life, so long as we get the tombstone in place?'

That's better, I thought. Mrs S. was feeling more like her old self again. With any luck, she wouldn't press me about the holiday.

'How was Jersey?' she asked.

'Oh, not bad,' I sighed. 'To tell the truth, I didn't see much of the island. Tied up in the hotel most of the time.'

'I've saved you the Smut,' said Mrs S. 'I don't suppose they allow it on to the island, do they?'

'I didn't see any,' I confessed.

In point of fact, the island must be the last resting place for every bit of paper that ever rolled off the presses in Fleet Street. Everywhere you looked, the newsstands were full of the F.T., the Wall Street Journal, the Financial Weekly and all that upper-class stuff. I was talking to the barman at the Grand who said the island was sinking under the weight of merchant banks and safe deposits. Lots of funny money there, too; you know, hot stuff from the Philippines and Hawaii, places like that. I wondered why Inspector Crozier, the well known Jersy detective, had not pulled in one or two blokes for questioning. Diplomatic immunity, I suppose. But, from what I hear, there are enough homegrown crooks on the island to keep him busy, anyway. You know, get-rich-quick merchants who are a bit shy about where their money came from and how much they've really got. They just put down a hundred grand on their tax returns and hope the taxman will believe them. Or so the barman said.

Come to think of it, I suppose I shall have to fill in a tax return now that I'm rich. In the old days, I never had to worry about anything like that. The boss did it for me through PAYE. But the rich are different. They not only have more money but have to explain where it came from. Of course, I hadn't been told to produce my accounts yet but I could see it looming on the horizon. Perhaps there was something to be said for keeping a little bit on the side in Jersey or the Isle of Man. After all, I'd be in good company.

I mentioned it to Freddy next time I saw him.

'Strictly speaking, it won't do you any good, old boy, unless you move abroad permanently,' he explained.

'Why's that?'

'Well,' said Freddy, 'so long as you're resident in the United Kingdom, it doesn't matter whether you earn money here or roll it up in the Bahamas, you will have to pay tax. The only way to avoid it is to live in the middle of the desert or somewhere.'

'I don't want to live in the desert.'

'In that case, you must get an accountant.'

'An accountant will keep the taxman at bay?'

'Absolutely,' said Freddy. 'Not one of these dodgy firms that will sell their grandmother down the river but a nice, respectable outfit that everyone thinks is as straight as a die.'

It was the old question of image again.

'As a matter of fact,' said Freddy, 'a friend of mine is just setting up in business. Why not give him a ring?'

'I thought you said I had to avoid dodgy firms?'

Freddy gave me a look that could only be described as pained.

'My dear Sid,' he replied, 'a respectable firm doesn't have to be a huge conglomerate with overheads that would make a strong man quake. It is ability that counts, not the superstructure.'

Freddy's friend did indeed lack the outward signs of material success. He had an office in Penge and seemed to be in the middle of painting it when I arrived.

'Didn't expect you so soon,' he said. 'Sit down.'

He removed the dust cover from a chair and indicated that, even in Penge, courtesy came first. He himself perched on the step ladder.

'You're my first client,' he said. 'I suppose I ought to offer you a discount.'

'You've never done this sort of thing before?' I asked.

'Not on my own account,' he said. 'I've been in practice for five years, one way or another.'

'You know all about tax havens and suchlike?'

'My dear sir, I know everything that is required to make your life a lot happier and your bank balance a lot healthier. Now, are you having trouble with the Revenue?'

'It's not flowing as well as I'd hoped,' I said.

A flicker of incomprehension crossed his brow. Then he forced a smile.

'No, the Revenue – the Inland Revenue. Is the taxman on your back?'

'Oh, I see! Well, not yet but I expect he soon will be.'

'Then we must take immediate steps to ensure that he doesn't get more than he is entitled.'

He wiped his hands on a bit of rag and blew the dust from the table.

'Now, how much are you worth?'

'I don't really know,' I said, thinking of the recent loss in Jersey and one or two unfortunate investments. 'About a million, I suppose.'

Freddy's friend – Brian, I discovered his name was – gave me a sharp look, as if to say, lying sod. But he restrained himself and continued.

'And where is this one million pounds, at the moment?' he asked politely.

'I don't really know that, either,' I said. 'I have about half a million invested and the rest is sort of lying around in various banks.'

'Tell me, sir, are you domiciled in this country?'

'I live here, if that's what you mean.'

'You wouldn't like to live for half the year in, say, Jersey or Nauru?'

'Not really,' I said.

'That's a pity because we could then put you out of harm's way for a while.'

He obviously doesn't know Jersey, I thought.

'What difference does it make?' I asked.

'Well, to be absolutely honest, it doesn't make as much difference as it used to when people like you had to pay 98 per cent on unearned income. Now you can keep more than half of it, legally.'

'So tax havens are redundant?' I asked.

'Let's say they're not as attractive as they used to be. But, of course, it's still better to pay twenty per cent rather than forty per cent.'

'Or nothing at all?' I said.

'I don't think I can manage that for you, sir – unless you would care to set up a trust company registered in, say, Liechtenstein?'

'Liechtenstein, eh?'

'Or Gibraltar. A friend of mine swears by Gibraltar. Puts all his gilt-edged business through a little firm there.'

'I don't fancy Gib.,' I said. 'Too close to the Costa del Crime.'

'There's always the Netherlands Antilles?'

'No, I'll stick to Britain, if you don't mind. Patriotism is the last refuge of the scoundrel.'

'As you wish, sir,' said my accountant, totting up an invisible sum. 'That means we shall have to work out something for you. What sort of income would you like?'

'As much as possible, of course.'

Brian looked at me as though I were a seven-year-old battling with the alphabet.

'Now, listen, Sid,' he said. 'I can see that you need a spot of advice. Anybody with a million quid doesn't have to worry about income, unless he's got a yacht and a couple of mistresses to maintain. What you need is capital growth.'

'And avoid income tax?' I said, seeing what he was driving at.

'Exactly. Buy a few shares, reap the rewards of other people's labour. Can't go wrong.'

'I already have some shares and they have gone wrong. I'm losing money on some of them.'

'Not to worry,' said Brian. 'We can use the losses to offset the gains. Keeps the tax down, you see.'

'Wouldn't it be better to make a lot of money and pay tax on it, rather than not make any just to keep it out of the hands of the taxman?'

'Of course,' said Brian. 'But we don't want to pay the government more than necessary. They'll only waste it.'

'What do you suggest, then?'

'Well, I think that for straight capital gain, you ought to commit a small sum – say, a quarter of a million – to the currency market. Let one of the foreign exchange boys see what he can do for you.'

'Let him gamble in foreign currencies, you mean?'

'I wouldn't say gamble. They trade, buying one currency and selling another. If you did if offshore, we could use one of the roll-up funds.'

'What does that mean?'

'It means that, if you make a profit, you won't have to pay tax until you bring the money home.'

'Sounds fair enough to me.'

'Tell you what, I'll have a friend of mine who's a foreign exchange dealer give you a ring. In the meantime, I'll look into your domestic liabilities, see if we can't reduce them.'

The thought of dabbling in foreign currencies appealed to me, I must admit. Ever since our trip to France, where a fistful of francs went a lot further than the same number of pounds, I had been struck by the possibilities. The only thing that slightly bothered me was that everybody kept talking about the strength of sterling. They were worried, it seemed, because the value of the old pounds, shilling and pence kept going up. In other words, instead of getting ten francs to the pound, you got eleven. But every so often some guy from the Labour Party or the CBI would come on the wireless and say we should have only nine. Didn't make sense to me. I mean, if the Japs and the Germans can make a bomb by having a strong currency, then why can't we in Britain? I decided to ask the broker when he rang.

'You can't really expect much else from the Labour Party, can you?' he said. 'They'll do anything, except work for a living.'

'I thought Labour was the party of the workers?' I said.

'Workers? Where have you been for the past half century, old son? The Labour Party is the party of ideals, not sordid manual toil. You won't find an overall or a grubby finger nail within a hundred miles of Walworth Road these days.'

'Does that mean that, if they ever get back into power, the pound will slump?' I asked.

'I'm glad you said "if",' said Barry (for that was his name).

'All right. Suppose the Social Democrats romp home. Would the pound slump then?'

'Not necessarily,' said Barry. 'It depends on what the market thinks of their policies.'

'So it could quite easily slump, even with the Tories in power?'

'Oh, quite,' said Barry. 'Again, it depends on the market's view.'

'So, it really doesn't matter which party is in power, the market will have the last word?'

'Exactly. You can't buck the market. Unless we join the snake, of course.'

'The snake will make a difference?'

'Not all the difference. But some difference. It restricts the ability of the market to move currencies up and down.'

'Isn't that a good thing?' I asked. 'Surely, a more stable currency market would be good for industry?'

(I'd heard the guy from the CBI rabbit on about that.)

'It would be good for industry but it wouldn't be so good for you or me.'

'Why not?'

'Because, old boy, if you want to make a few quid in the

foreign exchange market, you don't want the pound to sit there like a flea on a millpond. You want a bit of action, something to toss the market around. No movement, no profit.'

'I see.'

'You're catching on fast,' said Barry. 'You see, if we joined the snake, we might just as well pack up and go home. The central banks would impose their authority. No sudden squalls to catch the unwary with their pants down.'

'But how do you know which way the market will move?' I asked.

'Ah! That's where the skill of your broker comes in. Obviously, he's not going to put you in drachma while the Turks have got a glut of olive oil. But if we stick to the dollar we can virtually rely on a continuous crisis.'

'Sounds a bit risky to me,' I said.

'It's all risk, old boy. That's what makes the world go round. Get somebody who knows how to manage those risks and you're in the money. Get some jerk who ought to have retired at thirty and you're in the soup.'

I wondered how old Barry was but didn't like to ask.

'So, what would you like to do, sir? Invest a hundred on a discretionary basis or call the shots yourself?'

'I don't know anything about the currency market,' I admitted.

'In that case, you'll definitely need a manager. Just leave it to me, old son, and I'll have you in the supertax bracket before you can say Herstatt.'

'I was going to mention that,' I said. 'Is there any chance of doing it all offshore so that we can roll up the profits?'

'Reinvest them, you mean?' asked Barry.

'Yes, to keep them out the way of the taxman.'

There was a sharp intake of breath on the line.

'That's your business,' said my new investment adviser. 'I am but a simple foreign exchange dealer.'

I sensed that I had offended him somehow and decided not to pursue the matter.

'I'll put a cheque in the post,' I said.

'Righty-o, old boy. As soon as it's cleared, we'll start dealing for you.'

While I had been discussing the dollar, Mrs S. had been to the cemetery again. Mother was now in position and, with the blessing of the rabbi, a large block of stone had been placed on top of her. It would take more than a council official armed with an oil exploration licence to shift her next time.

'I notice they've taken the rig down at the municipal cemetery,' she said. 'Does that mean they've struck oil?'

'Could be,' I said. 'Or maybe they've given it up as a bad job.'

After a quick cup of tea, I got on the blower to the town hall. The one thing I've learned during my time in the City is that, to make money, you don't hang about. The bloke who is first with the news is usually first with the dough.

'I'm afraid you will have to phone the oil company, sir,' said the extremely helpful public servant at the other end of the line. 'It is their hole, not ours.'

The oil company was equally forthcoming.

'We don't release information about our drilling programme,' the exploration manager said.

'But I've got shares in your company,' I said. 'Surely the shareholders have a right to know?'

'We will advise the market in due course if there is anything to report. Otherwise I'm afraid I cannot help you.'

Surprisingly, Freddy saw their point of view.

'It doesn't look so good, though,' he added. 'If they'd struck hydrocarbons, they wouldn't have taken the rig away. They'd keep a crew there to cap the well.'

'Maybe I ought to have a look?' I suggested.

'Why not?' said Freddy. 'Take a bunch of flowers; pretend you're visiting relatives.'

Actually, pretence was unnecessary. When I got to the cemetery, or ex-cemetery as it then was, there was no sign of either the rig or a gusher.

'Well, you can't win 'em all,' said Freddy. 'Just as well you only had options.'

'How much is that down the drain, then?'

'I forget how many you bought. But it's probably no more than twenty grand.'

'Twenty grand?' I gulped.

'Well, it was your idea, old boy,' said Freddy, distancing himself from the deficit on current account.

I had to admit he was right. Investment is a tricky business, especially if you're punting in the dark. But I still had a chance. Now that the risk of methane had been removed, the builders would probably move in and put up millions of executive homes at a huge profit. Such is the nature of private enterprise.

'How is the Bongo loan coming along?' I asked, by way of interest.

'The Bongo loan?'

'Yes. The debt rescheduling exercise.'

'Oh, you'll have to ask Bernie about that,' said Freddy. 'He's in charge.'

'Ah, yes, well,' said Bernie, 'I'm afraid I have some bad news for you there, old son.'

'What kind of bad news?'

'Financial, mainly. Apparently, it wasn't Bongo that wanted a new loan to pay off its debts. It was some place in South America – you know, where the generals have a bit of clout in Washington.'

'So, what does that mean?' I asked, my throat unusually dry.

'It means, I'm afraid, that you own half a million quid's worth of Bongo bonds that are worth no more than they were a couple of weeks ago.'

'Let's get rid of them, then. Put the money into something more profitable.'

'I could try to sell them, I suppose,' said Bernie. 'Not much demand for that sort of stock, though. If I were you, I'd hang on in the hopes that somebody – the froggies, maybe – comes along with a guilty conscience and bails 'em out.'

'But that might take years,' I said.

'Could well do,' Bernie agreed. 'And we have to accept the possibility that it may never happen.'

'And so I'm stuck with a load of worthless paper?'

'Put it this way, old boy. You're in very good company. Some of the biggest banks in the world have got their vaults stuffed full of it. You can rest assured that they'll be rooting on your behalf.'

'But the banks can afford it. I can't.'

'Tell you what,' said Bernie, 'as it was partly my fault for getting the wires crossed, I'll forego my commission. How about that?'

'That's very kind of you,' I said not wishing to appear ungrateful, 'but how much am I losing on the deal?'

'In theory, you're not losing anything at the moment. It's just that you have an asset that would be extremely difficult to sell.'

'But I can't be the only person in the world who would want to buy Bongo stock?'

'You are certainly a very special type of investor,' Bernie said. 'But don't worry. The Bongo-wongas might end up having to buy their own stock, just to clear the shelves, so to speak. You'd be guaranteed a market then.'

Brian, my new accountant, totted up the figures when I consulted him in Penge the following day.

'Well, you could be a lot worse off,' he said. 'And you're lucky, in a way. At least you can afford to lose a few quid without worrying about the roof over your head.'

We set about trying to establish what Brian called my 'net worth'. Apparently, that's how you described your financial position today. Individuals of high net worth were those who could always get a loan from the bank. Those with a low, or negative, net worth were likely to stay that way, unless they won the pools.

Brian spread a copy of the Financial Times on his desk and switched on his calculator.

'We'll take the negative factors first,' he said.

(That, I gathered, was a polite way of describing losses attributable to the investment strategy of others.)

'I think that, to be prudent, we should write off the investment in Bongo bonds. Unless, of course, we can find some idiot to take them on.'

He depressed the key that immediately flashed up a minus fifty thou. on the digital display unit.

'Then there are the options on Cemetery Oil. I'm afraid there's nothing to salvage there, unless they strike oil somewhere else in the next couple of days, and that's unlikely. I'm afraid we must assume that the options will expire without any profit to yourself.'

He added twenty grand to the minus figure. I had always thought that two negatives made a positive. They don't. They just make a bigger negative.

'And then there's Euro Jaunts. Pity about that.'

The calculator showed an overall loss of £100,000.

'Now we'll see what the Synthetic is worth.'

He ran his eye over the prices in the F.T. and made a note in the margin.

'Pity you didn't buy a few more ICI,' he said. 'They're doing quite nicely.'

By the time he had gone through the entire portfolio of high-yielding blue chips the leaded light was showing a plus figure of £250,000.

'And you reckon you've got about half a million in various bank accounts?'

'About that.'

In fact, that was not quite accurate. I remembered the £100,000 I had just committed to the foreign exchange market.

'At the moment, we can probably still regard that as an asset,' said Brian. 'But, don't forget, a balance sheet simply reflects your financial position at the time it was drawn up. We could produce a very nice statement and – bingo! the market crashes and it's a pack of lies.'

'I think it's a fairly accurate statement of my net worth at this precise moment in time,' I said. 'Unless the market has taken another tumble this morning.'

'We'll assume it's correct,' said Brian. 'But you really must keep a grip on your expenses. You can't just nip in and out of the market on a whim.'

'They're not whims,' I said. 'They're the recommendations of my broker.'

He stared at the visual display unit and scratched the back of his neck.

'How much did you say you had won?'

I told him.

'Well, I reckon you're about two hundred grand down at the moment. Not so good, sir, if you look at it objectively.'

It was not so good whichever way you looked at it. But the figures simply did not add up. I know that accountants can do wonderful things (which is why I had hired one) but even Brian could not make £100,000 disappear into thin air. Then I remembered the loose change under Mrs S.'s mattress. However, I did not confide in my accountant. There are some things that even a financial consultant should not know about.

'You must have had a bit of a spending spree,' said Brian. 'What was her name?'

'Cheryl,' I said. 'How did you know?'

'Intuition,' said Brian. 'Don't worry. I'll put it down as business expenses. The important thing is that we've established a nice capital loss with no income to compensate. The taxman will be hard pressed to screw anything out of you on that.'

8. Flight into quality

'I think you should get yourself a proper adviser,' said Mrs S. when I reported my net worth to her that evening.

I don't know why I felt obliged to tell her but I did. After all, she knew how much I had won and, apart from a month's rent in advance and a tombstone for Mother, she had not had anything much. A golddigger from Huddersfield she was not.

'Perhaps you're right,' I said, 'although, if it hadn't have been for Freddy, the banks would have had a million quid free of charge.'

'All the same, it wouldn't do any harm to have a word with the manager and explain the situation,' said Mrs S. 'They must have somebody on the staff who knows about stocks and shares. And don't forget you've got nine banks. You can have nine different lots of advice, if you like.'

As usual, Mrs S. had hit the nail on the head. To remain a millionaire – even in our go-getting society which had thrown off the shackles of financial restraint – was proving more difficult than I had imagined. Perhaps a quiet word with the manager wouldn't do any harm. But which manager? All nine, as Mrs S. had suggested, or one who could speak for them all? Mirror, mirror, on the wall, who gives the fairest advice of all? The mirror was no help so I decided to plump for efficiency. I made an appointment with my German bank.

My first surprise was to discover that the manager was not one of those crew-cut krauts you see in the war comics but a gentleman of what might be called the old school. He didn't actually say that he was an Aryan soul, educated at Gordonstoun, and that I was a member of the proletariat who lived with the former Miss Rosenbaum. But, there again, he didn't have to. I got the message that, had I not won the pools, he would not have bothered to pass the time of day.

'Villi Valdorf,' he said, shaking hands and offering me a pew. 'What can I do for you.'

'I came for a spot of advice,' I said, wondering whether it had been such a good idea after all.

'What sort of advice?' he asked, raising a Teutonic eyebrow.

'I don't seem to be having much luck on the Stock Exchange,' I said. 'My broker makes more in commission than I do in profit.'

'The omens are certainly unfavourable,' he said. 'But I always think that investment should not depend on luck, don't you? What it should depend on is sound advice from somebody who knows the market and is prepared to take the long view, rather than the short one.'

'Exactly,' I said.

Perhaps he wasn't such a bad chap, after all.

'Who is your broker?' he asked.

I told him.

'I think,' said Villi, 'that we have probably identified the cause of your misfortune. Might I suggest that you transfer your business to the bank? I'm sure we could do better than your friend Bernie.'

'You can pick the winners, can you?'

'My dear sir, we have probably the best team of security analysts in London.' Leaning forward and addressing the intercom, he added: 'Bring me the latest investment bulletin, will you, Miss Abergombe?'

Miss Abergombe, a refugee from either Idi Amin or the Ethiopian famine, or perhaps both, arrived in about five seconds flat.

'A descendant of Haille Selassie, you know,' said Villi, noting my interest. 'Very efficient, in all manner of things.'

He handed me the document. Now, if there's one thing I don't understand about the City, it's a report written by a securities analyst. A report written by two analysts and an economist for a German bank might just as well be in double Dutch. I tried to look impressed.

'We, of course, are one of the few banks not to have our own broker,' said Villi. 'We take the view, which is very unfashionable now, I know, that a bank ought to be separated from the securities market – and not just by a Chinese wall. Avoids any potential conflict of interest, you know.'

'Quite,' I said.

The only conflict of interest I knew was between the amount paid out to buy shares and the amount that came back when they were sold. I wondered how the Chinese got into the act.

'Yes,' continued Villi, 'we do not subscribe to the theory that bankers and brokers will be more efficient if they sleep in the same bed. We believe that the interests of the client will be better served if the broker, or market maker, does not have to worry about the bank's position.'

'It seems to me,' he added, his blue blood throbbing at his temples, 'that we are forgetting the lessons of the Great Crash of 1929. The banks, I regret to say, were largely responsible for fuelling the boom that led up to that crash – and the Depression that followed. Too much easy credit. Congress, quite rightly, decided to impose some controls and separate the activities of banks and brokers. It is a pity that your own government, in its haste to deregulate the markets and please its friends in the City, has ignored the Glass-Steagall Act.'

Well, to be quite honest, I hadn't a clue what he was talking about. As far as I could make out, he didn't like the idea of banks being in the stockbroking business. If he had a broker like mine, I'm not surprised. He noticed the frown on my forehead.

'You see, Mr Arbuthnot,' he said, 'we believe that only by standing outside the market can we give objective advice. We are not going to talk our book – because we haven't got a book. So that's why you may rest assured that any advice you receive from the bank will be entirely free of vested interest.'

He smiled. They certainly know how to bring up gents at Gordonstoun. I wondered if I should put my name down and reserve a place for my kids, if I ever had any. I made a mental note to ask Mrs S. to ring the school and find out how much they required as a deposit.

'What about life assurance and unit trusts?' I asked. 'Can you advise me there, too?'

'Of course,' said Villi. 'We do not accept commissions from either unit trusts or life assurance companies. If you want our advice on these matters, then we may charge you a fee –

depending on how good a customer you are,' he added.

Even I could see the advantage of that. I know that some of these life insurance salesmen earn a bomb. You've only got to let 'em get a foot in the door and you've got all the policies you'll ever need. They promise half the gold in Fort Knox – if only you live long enough and the stock market doesn't crash in the meantime. And I've often thought when seeing some of the flash cars that salesmen drive, 'Who's paying for that, then?'. I mean, the money has got to come from somewhere, hasn't it? And if it all goes on petrol and expenses you're not going to get much back, are you? Not only that, but a lot of these salesmen have taken to calling themselves financial counsellors and suchlike. I know they've got to be licensed and are not supposed to pull the wool over your eyes but what happens if they're short of a quid or two at the end of the week? They're not going to be too fussy about the advice they give, are they? They're gonna bung you in the policy that pays the biggest commission. That means their roast beef on Sunday comes from your pocket, old son.

I must admit, though, that although Villi appeared legal, decent and honest and not at all like some folks in the City, I was a bit out of my depth. I had a nasty feeling that his advice might come on the expensive side.

'You have enough life assurance, I assume?' he said, bringing the conversation back to a practical level.

'I've never got around to it, I'm afraid,' I confessed.

Villi was shocked, and possibly genuinely horrified.

'My dear sir!' he exclaimed. 'You really must do something about that. Suppose you were to be run over by a bus when you left the office here? How would your dependents manage to live' – he glanced casually at the state of my account – 'on a mere one hundred thousand pounds?'

'I've got a lot more in other bank accounts,' I replied.

'You have other bank accounts?'

For the first time, I noticed a slight German accent creep into Villi's voice. It was his turn to frown.

'Oh, yes, I've got half a dozen or so accounts, scattered here and there.'

'Why so many?' asked Villi. 'Is not the bank here good enough for you?'

'I just like to spread the risk' I said, remembering what one of my unpaid advisers had said about banks going bust.

Villi glanced at his watch. I had a feeling that the meter had run out of free time.

'I think I really ought to make an appointment for you to see our client services manager,' he said. 'He'll arrange for you to be properly insured and perhaps suggest a few shares – German companies have a very good track record, you know.'

He stood up. When a kraut from Gordonstoun stands up and extends his hand, you know the interview is over, even though you are about to pay him a fee for the benefit of his impartial and totally objective advice.

'I'll have Miss Abergombe arrange a mutually convenient time for you to meet Mr Wellemeyer,' he said (although, of course, it came out like Vellemeyer). 'In the meantime, do take our circular on the growth of the money supply. I'm sure you'll find our research very thorough. Good day to you.'

Strangely enough, Mrs S. seemed a lot happier to know that I might have to pay for the privilege of knowing what insurance policy to buy.

'You know what they say – you get what you pay for,' she reminded me, cutting a slice of Grandmother's Very Own Gingerbread, made to a traditional recipe. 'That's why the rich always get richer. They can afford professional advice.'

'I'm rich – but I seem to be getting poorer,' I said. 'Anyway, insurance companies are all much of a muchness You've only got to look in the paper. They all offer a fantastic deal, unless you've got Aids.'

'If they were all the same,' asked Mrs S., 'why would people go to the bother of paying somebody to tell them which was the best one?'

Until I had met Villi, it was not a question to which I had ever given much thought.

'I mean,' said Mrs S., rubbing salt into the wound, 'just look what's happened to your investments so far, thanks to your friend Bernie's advice. That didn't cost you anything and a fat lot of good it has done you.'

She was right, of course. My Auntie Ivy used to say that you get owt for nowt, which I think meant that there is no such thing as a free lunch. (Not that I had had many free lunches just lately. The rule seemed to be: if Sid's got his cheque book, let him pay.) But, when you come to think of it, both Mrs S. and Aunty Ivy were right. Why are the rich rich? Why do they never buy their insurance from a bloke with his foot in the door and a BMW double-parked in the street? Why do they employ a small army of lawyers, accountants and other professional advisers? I don't know but they must reckon it's worth their while.

I told Freddy I had been having serious thoughts about my investment strategy next time I saw him. In particular, I told him that I was thinking of paying for some proper advice. He seemed very hurt.

'Well, I won't claim that Bernie is the best broker in the world,' he said with commendable frankness, 'but I will say this: you won't have to pay him a fee every time you want to know whether ICI has paid a dividend or not. He'll check for you in two shakes of a horse's tail.'

'But you must admit,' I countered, 'that his advice hasn't been very profitable so far.'

'Now, be fair, old boy,' said Freddy, pouring himself another glass of claret. 'You did very well out of Northern Puds.'

'Only because some Arab came to the rescue. Your Euro Jaunts turned out to be a dead loss.'

'Unfortunate, unfortunate,' said Freddy. 'But, to be frank, I don't think you gave 'em a fair go.'

'What about Bongo bonds? I thought bonds were supposed to be safer than shares?'

'Depends what sort of bonds,' said Freddy. 'Some bonds are safer than others. For instance, if you'd have backed the Tsar at the time of the revolution, you'd have only just got your money back.'

'But the Russians don't believe in capitalism. Bongo does.'

'Don't you believe it, old boy. They've got some of the sharpest brains in the business. Just look at the way they took the Americans for a ride over all that wheat a few years ago.'

He paused.

'Of course, if you really want a bit of action and a chance to make a quick buck you ought to sink a few quid in commodities.'

'What sort of commodities?' I asked.

'Oh, anything really,' said Freddy. 'It was the wheat that made me think of it.'

'But I don't want a truckload of wheat. I've got nowhere to store it.'

'But you don't have to take delivery of it – that's the beauty of the futures market.'

'What are futures?' I asked.

'Well, they're sort of commodities that don't actually exist,' said Freddy. 'You just bet – well, not exactly bet – you try to guess what the price will be in, say, three months time and put your money where your mouth is. Very profitable, if you get it right.'

'What happens if you get it wrong?'

'Tell you what,' said Freddy, 'I've got a friend who's a commodity broker. I'll introduce you, if you like, and vouch for your net worth.'

'Can't Bernie do it?' I asked.

''Fraid not,' said Freddy. 'Different sort of broker, different sort of market.'

He finished his claret.

'Don't know why I didn't think of it before,' he said.

I can't say I liked Siggy, the commodities broker. Of all the blokes I had met in the City so far, he was the smoothest. I mean, even though Villi Valdorf and I were in a different class, eugenically speaking, we could both appreciate a bit of dark-skinned crumpet when we saw it. And even though old Freddy was a bit fond of drinking my claret and always rushing off before he could buy a bottle himself, I had a soft spot for him. (So had Mrs S., I noticed. Her attitude had softened considerably while I had been in Jersey.) But this guy from the 'commission house' (I think Freddy called it) was somehow different.

For a start, he wore an extremely expensive suit. I could tell that because my old man had worked for a tailor at one stage and used to come home with samples now and again; never more than a yard at a time but enough to give a young lad like me a feeling for the right stuff. Siggy's shoes didn't come from Dolcis, either. More like Russell and Bromley, on a special last. But it was his manner that got me. It wasn't like Villi's, who let you know as politely as possible that one shouldn't judge the Prussian aristocracy by a little corporal from Vienna, but sort of calculating. I had the feeling that I was about to be ripped off the moment I stepped inside his office and he gave me a piece of paper to sign.

'What's this, then?' I asked.

'Oh, just a declaration saying that you know what you're doing,' said Siggy, not hiding his contempt for the nouveau riche.

'But I don't know what I'm doing,' I said. 'I've never dealt in commodities before.'

'That doesn't really matter,' said Siggy, 'so long as you appreciate that there are risks involved and that commodity trading is not for widows and orphans.'

'You mean, you can lose money at it?'

'You can lose money on anything,' said Siggy, shrugging his well-cut shoulders. 'Even houses go down in value from time to time.'

'And what if I don't sign?'

'Then I'm afraid I won't be able to deal for you.'

Well, there it was. Straight on the line. No signature, no deal. It was a pity to have come all this way just to learn that. I scrawled my signature in the blank space under the small print. As Siggy snatched it away, I noticed it was headed 'Risk disclosure statement'.

'I think,' said Siggy, relaxing a little, 'that the most profitable way to go about this is for me to trade on a discretionary basis. That means I can keep an eye on things for you and take instant decisions.'

'You go to the market every day, do you?'

He gave me a positively withering look. I realised too late that commodity brokers do not grub around in buckets of hogwash and the like.

'Nowadays, it's done on the screen,' he explained patiently. 'I couldn't keep an eye on everything if I had to cover all the markets, spot as well as terminal.'

'I suppose not,' I said.

'What would you like to kick off with?' asked Siggy, opting for the terminal on his desk. 'Metals or one of the softs?'

'How about coffee?' I said.

He pressed a button.

'Coffee's limit up at the moment. Besides, I don't like either the fundamental position or the charts. Three months Arabica has been looking very vulnerable for some time and the latest report from Parana puts the temperature well above average with not even a hint of frost. I'd go for something more volatile, if I were you.'

Well, if Siggy had been trying to impress me with his knowledge of the market, he had certainly succeeded. If, on the other hand, he had been trying to baffle me with science, he had succeeded there, too.

'I thought frost would be bad for the coffee crop?' I said. 'Wouldn't it kill the plants?'

'It would, indeed, sir. But that's what we want in the commodities market – some bad news to make the price go up. Nice warm tropical nights only lead to a glut.'

The theory of commodity trading suddenly lay bare before me. At a glance, I could see how exciting it was. Now I know what Freddy meant when he spoke of action.

'I suppose that what we need is something in short supply,' I said, warming to the idea. 'Shortage always makes the price go up, doesn't it?'

'In theory, yes,' agreed Siggy. 'But, of course, you don't have to buy. You could sell.'

'But I haven't go anything to sell,' I protested.

'Perhaps I ought to explain the futures market to you,' said Siggy, adopting the role of a professional adviser. 'You see, in the futures market you don't have to own any coffee or cocoa or whatever. You just buy a contract or sell a contract – whichever you think will make money. You don't have to worry about shiploads of soyabeans or anything like that.'

'But I haven't even got a contract,' I said.

Siggy sighed. He was obviously dealing with an idiot.

'My dear Sid, that doesn't matter. You just find somebody who wants to buy a contract and sell it to him. I can very soon write you a contract. It's only a piece of paper.'

For the first time, I noticed a small cloud drifting across the otherwise clear blue sky of the commodities market. I had been caught out with bits of paper before. Witness one worthless Bongo bond. When it came to the crunch, bits of paper were not as valuable as, say, bits of gold.

'What about gold?' I asked. 'Couldn't you just buy me a bar to keep under the bed?'

'A bar of gold?'

'Yes, a bar.'

'I'm afraid that what you need there is a bullion dealer,' said Siggy. 'I'm a commodity trader. I don't deal in gold.'

'But I thought gold was a commodity?'

'So it is, so it is. But we're not talking about gold bars, we're talking about the futures market.'

'Bits of paper?'

'Quite. I could buy you a gold contract on Comex, if you like, although the metal seems very reluctant to move at the moment. The currency markets are too quiet.'

'Not enough turbulence, eh?'

I didn't like to tell him that I had a hundred grand waiting for a sudden squall to toss a few pennies my way.

'No. Gold always does best when people are frightened of losing their shirts. I wouldn't buy – at least, not until we have a full-blown balance of payments crisis.'

'What about cocoa?' I asked. 'Is that any good?'

Siggy pressed a button with a resigned shrug.

'Pretty quiet there, really. Nothing much happening since rust was brought under control. We could always hope for a punch-up among the Swiss, I suppose. But that would be taking a risk.'

He zapped through the markets with the consummate skill of

a professional.

'Now, what about orange juice?' he asked. 'I did hear a rumour that the Mafia had cornered the market in Europe. That should give our friends in the Middle East something to think about.'

'How would that affect the futures market?'

'Don't you see? He who controls the supply of orange juice can charge what he likes. The price would go through the roof.'

'But I thought oranges were in over-supply, like beetroot and cauliflowers?'

'You should not under-estimate the business acumen of the family,' said Siggy. 'They need a fairly substantial cash flow to disguise income from other sources, if you see what I mean.'

I didn't, but I thought it wise not to give Siggy the impression that I was a complete novice in what was obviously a very complex business.

'Why not just leave it to me?' he asked, getting impatient again. 'I'll see that you're switched in and out at the right time. How much would you like to commit to the market?'

Looking back, I suppose that was one of the little phrases that ought to have alerted me to the dangers of speculating in commodities. Not 'How much would you like to invest?'. But 'How much would you like to commit to the market?'. If I had been a seafarer, I might also have been struck by the similarity of Siggy's words and those of the ship's chaplain when he puts on his surplice and intones, 'We hereby commit this body (of some old dear who had died of heat stroke in the Red Sea) to the deep'. But, at the time, I thought it was just a bit more of the jargon – something to impress Mrs S. with.

'Why don't we start with a hundred thousand and see how things go?' I said.

'Fine,' said Siggy. 'I should be able to do something with that.'

I left him with two cheques: one drawn on my Arab account, the other on my Far Eastern assets. After all, commodities – or contracts, as Siggy kept referring to them – were an exotic business. It was only right that they should be financed with exotic cheques.

I was surprised, to say the least, when Siggy phoned a couple of days later and asked for some more money.

'The market is against you, I'm afraid,' he said. 'Three months copper has not performed as well as I'd hoped.'

'But I thought I was in orange juice?' I said.

'You were – but I had to switch or risk losing a potential upswing in non-ferrous metals,' he explained. 'Unfortunately, the latest U.S. stockpile figures were a lot healthier than anticipated. You'll have to put up another ten thou. or be bombed out.'

'Does that mean I've lost all my money?' I asked, with a tongue like sandpaper on a dry day in the desert.

'Not if you put up enough to keep the contract alive,' said Siggy. 'But if I have to sell you out you can probably write off your initial investment.'

'I thought you were going to look after me and make sure my fingers didn't get burned?' I said, beginning to get niggled.

'I am looking after you,' said Siggy. 'That's why I need some more cash to keep us afloat.'

'All right,' I said. 'I'll send you another ten grand. But you'll have to get by on that until the dividends start rolling in.'

'Okay,' said Siggy. 'But send it round on a bike. I'll need it by the end of the day.'

Despite the excitement of buying soyabeans in Chicago and selling coffee on Comex (an excitement dimmed only by the unexpected request for an extra £10,000), I felt that something was missing in the commodities game. What I really wanted, and in this I shared the feelings of many primitive peoples, like the Indians and Chinese, was a bar of gold that I could call my very own. Gold was a store of value – a visible sign of wealth that you could stuff in your teeth and impress your friends with. It was, I suppose, a dental version of a Porsche. I was determined to have a bar, despite what any of my financial advisers might say.

I took a taxi to the City and asked the driver if he knew of a bullion dealer. He pulled up in some back street and pointed to a hole in the wall.

'You go in there and ask for Les,' he said, fumbling for the change. 'I've got a few Krugers, myself, like. Had 'em for years now. Trouble is, they don't pay dividends.'

'You can't have everything,' I said, trying to sound knowledgeable. 'There is a price for security and peace of mind.'

'Quite right, guv.,' he said, touching his forelock in response to my £1 tip.

Les turned out to be very helpful. You could see at a glance that he was one of these blokes they call a gold bug. He rattled on for about five minutes before tumbling to the fact that I wanted a bar to take away, here and now. That threw him.

'I'm afraid we haven't got any gold here,' he said. 'We only trade in the stuff.'

'But, surely, if you buy and sell, you must know where I could get some?'

Les looked thoughtful. He turned to one of his offsiders.

'Where could we get a bar of gold at this time of day?' he asked.

'Zurich?' said his mate, helpfully.

'But surely you've got some in the vaults?' I persisted.

'I'm not sure,' said Les, playing it cool. I guess he had heard of the great Brinks Mat heist. 'Depends how much you want.'

'I only want one bar.'

'Kilo or full size?'

'You know, one of the big ones.'

Les punched a few figures into his calculator.

'If we've got one – and I'm not saying we have – it'll cost you £120,000.'

The enthusiasm I had felt when Les had spoken of 'the flight into quality' and 'the bullshit surrounding SDRs' waned ever so slightly as I contemplated an investment on this scale.

'I just wanted something to keep under the bed,' I said.

Les placed a friendly hand on my shoulder and gave it to me straight between the eyes.

'Listen,' he said. 'What the hell do you want a bar of gold for? You're not a jeweller, are you? I'll sell you a bar, all right, but you'll have to pay 15 per cent VAT. That's 15 per cent down the drain straight away. Why not take out a gold contract on

Comex? It'll be a lot cheaper.'

I thanked Les for his help. He was the first person in London actually to turn down my business. As a result, I was £15,000 better off than I would have been had I bought a bar of gold and helped to subsidise the Customs and Excise canteen. It's a pity Les was merely a bullion dealer and not my financial adviser.

'By the way,' said Mrs S. when I got home, 'a Miss Abergombe rang.'

'Oh, yes,' I said. 'She probably wants to make an appointment.'

'Are you sure it's not the other way around?' asked Mrs S., spitefully. 'Sounded to me as though she might run a massage parlour.'

'That's just her sexy African voice,' I said, sensing the jealousy of an Older Woman. 'I don't suppose she massages anything more exciting than a few figures at the bank.'

'That's all right, then,' said Mrs S.

I wouldn't have minded falling into the hands of Miss Abergombe, I must admit, but the thought of meeting Mr Vellemeyer to discuss life assurance made the eyes glaze over. Mr Vellemeyer, however worthy his advice, was unlikely to provide the sort of stimulation that a millionaire required at the end of a long week.

I decided that before ringing Miss Abergombe and making an appointment I would have a short holiday. The jaunt to Jersey had been extremely wearing on the nerves and, as far as Mrs S. was concerned, had been a business trip, anyway. With my investments under control, I could afford a few days off. I decided to go to Germany so that, when I returned, I could talk to the krauts on their own level.

9. Donner und blitzen

The first thing you notice about the Germans is that they don't sprecken ze English. Sure, you can get by at the hotel where they train the staff to speak basic American (and probably Russian, in case glasnost doesn't work). But once you're among the locals, in the beer kellars and pretzel gardens, you've got to have a phrase book or they won't know what you're on about. Hopefully, it will all be different in 1992 when the old Union Jack will be fluttering over half the factories in the Ruhr.

I stayed at a big, posh hotel in Frankfurt, overlooking the River Main. I decided on Frankfurt because the guy at the German Tourist Office said it was the financial capital of the nation. Apparently, the Rothschild family began their long climb up the social ladder from here and so that was another point in its favour. If they could do it, so could I. From what I gather, they had only a few quid and a barrow load of bananas to start with. Look at 'em now, though! You wouldn't think they were Jewish.

What I really wanted to study, though, was the thinking behind the economic miracle that had filled the streets of Britain with Mercedes and BMWs. Not the ecological cost of the miracle – I mean, we all know that factories kill a few fish occasionally – but the philosophy that makes the krauts work twice as hard any anybody else. I figured that Frankfurt would be the ideal spot to absorb the economic atmosphere without breathing in too much of the industrial air. I asked the guy at the reception desk to book me a tour of the city.

'Certainly, sir. Would you like a day trip embracing our cultural heritage or a tour of the night spots?'

I suppose I ought to have said culture but a bloke of my background, even if he is a millionaire, doesn't want to know any more about this bird called Clara Schumann, who apparently kicked the bucket there some years ago, than he already knows. So I plumped for the night spots.

'As you wish, sir. When would you like to go? Tonight?'

'Why not?'

Well, I thought, if friend Vellemeyer at the bank turns out to be half as efficient as his fellow countryman at the hotel I might put all my investments his way. The guy didn't even ask me to pay for the tour in advance, unlike Siggy, of three-month copper fame. At eight o'clock, a wagon turned up at the hotel and I heard them paging Mr Arbuthnot.

Mr Arbuthnot, who was feeling a bit peckish by then, was down the stairs in a flash. Mind you, the wagon did look a bit like a black maria (the sort used to take soccer fans to the gas chambers), except that it was blue. The reason for its size, I soon discovered, was that other visitors also preferred clubs to culture. Several tourists were already waiting. Mostly blokes, though. In fact, all blokes.

'Ve vill,' said the driver, jumping behind the veel, 'take you on a tour of the night spots of Frankfort. Ve vill haf you back at your hotels by midnight, unless you vish to make other arrangements.'

He drove off down the autobahn, stopping once or twice to pick up more customers, while we sat in the back and waited. I sat next to an Arab – not one of the rich Arabs with a Christmas pud factory in his portfolio but a funny little guy from Morocco. They don't have much of a night life in their own country, I suppose, and make the most of it when they get away from the village. As I don't speak Moroccan and he didn't speak English, we didn't have much to say to each other. The only guy who spoke English was a loud-mouthed Yank and I didn't fancy chatting to him. Reminded me too much of a vacuum-cleaner salesman. So, apart from Ehrich babbling on as we rattled over the cobbles, it was all pretty quiet. Spooky, really, considering we were supposed to be having a night out on the town. Even when we arrived at the beer kellar and had one of the sausages for which the city is famous, the Moroccan just grinned into his orange juice. Moslem, I suppose.

Well, to cut a long story short, we eventually piled out for the highlight of the evening. We were in the old town at what Ehrich said was an old brewery. It looked more like a nuclear shelter to me. All these steps led down to what appeared to be just a hole in the ground. Ehrich said it was a restaurant, with night club and cabaret. By that time, I'd had a skinful of beer at the pubs we'd stopped at and almost fell flat on my face. Hank, my American friend – he wasn't so bad when you came to know him – grabbed hold of me and held me upright.

'Take it easy, old son,' he said.

Down the bottom, in the bowels of the earth, it was pretty posh and jolly expensive. I wondered how the little Moroccan would explain that to his missus. But I could see that most of the other people there were in the same financial class as myself. They may not have been Rothschilds but they were not short of a bob or two. Fat, balding old blokes who looked as if they might have done well out of the thaw in relations between East and West. Surprisingly, most of them had their wives with them. At least, I assumed that the women were their wives. They were a bit too old for dolly birds. But I suppose it takes all sorts to make a world and if you've been bashing metal all day long to weld an economic miracle you haven't got time to chase the floozies.

Do you remember what Bernard Shaw said about human nature being incurably depraved? He actually gave it the benefit of the doubt. But it was clear, as soon as the lights dimmed and the cabaret came on, that he had never been to Frankfurt. Let me say first of all that I am mightily glad there was no cabaret at that French joint where Mrs S. and I spent a frustrating evening. I would not have known where to hide my face. Here, in Frankfurt, they had obviously rounded up a few members of the cast of Oh! Calcutta! and shoved 'em on the stage without bothering to kit 'em out first at the Army surplus stores. Starkers! Every one of them! Blokes as well as birds. I won't say much about the birds except to note that they were not the sort you would normally find on Page Three. They were sagging in all the wrong places. The blokes were a bit saggy, too, as though prancing around like that hadn't done 'em much good (which it probably hadn't). But that didn't seem to worry my friend, the Moroccan. He got quite excited and kept patting my knee. For a moment, I thought he might be queer.

Actually, I was more interested in the reactions of the burger masters and their wives as it was them that I had come to study. They all looked bored stiff, as though they had seen it all before. Perhaps they had. But, if it was that interesting, why come again? Perhaps they just liked being seen in the right places. You know, night club one night, dinner party with friends the next. Anything to get you up the social scale. Mind you, if you ran into the Chancellor at a place like this you'd go down the greasy pole with a bump, I reckon. How anybody responsible for an economic miracle could enjoy a show like this, I don't know. Worse than the Daily Smut, and that is saying something. I was glad when it was over and Ehrich said it was time to go back to the hotel. I made sure I sat well away from the Moroccan in the coach. But I needn't have worried. He was sitting next to some Danish bloke, just grinning.

Frankfurt, I discovered, is not the place that you would go to willingly on holiday. Sure, they've got a lot of culture and apple strudl but you soon get tired of that. Fortunately, I had an ulterior motive – to find out how the krauts managed to have the strongest currency and the lowest interest rates in Europe. From what I read in the F.T., that took some doing. In Britain, it would be an economic miracle, all right.

After lunch, I decided to do some window shopping. I wondered what to take Mrs S. as a present from the industrial heart of Europe. She seemed a bit put out that I had not invited her along but you can't take your landlady everywhere, can you, especially to a soft porn dive that calls itself a night club. Besides, I wanted to have a decco at my German bank, which was based here. To judge by the calibre of kraut they employed in London, it was bound to be an impressive place – although not one that would have held much interest for Mrs S.

As I strolled along, none too slowly because of an autumnal nip in the air, I became aware of a disturbance. A huge crowd of people were pushing and shoving outside one of the commercial buildings. At first, I thought they were students. You know how they go on at times; worse than Millwall fans. But these people seemed a lot older. Some of them were getting quite hot under the collar, yammering on and waving bits of paper around. I couldn't work out what they were saying because, although I had managed to pick up a couple of words, I wouldn't say that I was fluent in German. When the cops arrived, I decided it was time to leave. I've seen these German cops in action. They're not trained to respect the person as are the boys in blue back home. You not only get a crack over the head with a baton but have to engage in unarmed combat with a hungry Alsatian. I turned diplomatically and walked swiftly back to the hotel. Mrs S. would have to go without a prezzy.

The first intimation that all was not well in the financial capital of Germany came the following morning when I checked out. The bloke at the desk turned quite pale as I wrote out a cheque, drawn on the local bankhaus.

'Have you not read the papers this morning, sir?' he enquired.

'My landlady is probably keeping them for me,' I replied.

'What I meant was, have you not read the reports on all the front pages about your bank?'

'What about my bank?' I said, sensing that something was wrong.

'A question of balance, I believe,' the kraut said, speaking quite good English. 'I'm afraid that we cannot accept this cheque.'

'Cannot accept a cheque?'

'Not this cheque, sir.'

'Look here, my good man,' I said, remembering who had won the war. 'It's a bit much if a German company can't accept a German cheque, especially as you've only got to walk down the street to cash it.'

'That is just the point, sir. I don't think we would be able to cash it. I suggest you read the papers.'

'Don't worry, I will,' I said. 'And I'll have a word with the manager when I get home.'

'In the meantime, sir, how are you going to settle your account?'

'Just send the bill to the British consul,' I said irritably.

'That would not do any good, sir. In the past, he has just sent them back again.'

'Will you take Barclaycard?'

'Of course.'

Now, it seemed to me as I made my way to the airport that something was very rotten in the state of Frankfurt. For some reason, German banks had suddenly gone out of fashion. I had a feeling that those people in the street yesterday knew more than they had let on. As soon as I landed at Heathrow, I looked for a phone box that didn't need a Phonecard and dialled Miss Abergombe at the bank. Eventually, I was connected to a recorded message.

'This is the London office of the West Deutsche Blitzen und Handels Krieg. We are sorry but the office is closed until further notice. For urgent enquiries concerning your account, please telephone the receivers, Messrs. Fork and Sully.'

Receivers? What about Villi? What about Miss Abergombe? What about the hundred thousand quid, sitting in the vault, that Mr Vellemeyer was going to invest for me? German companies, I kept telling myself, did not go bust in the middle of the day, when a bloke was in Frankfurt to study the economic miracle. They were part of the social and economic fabric. I tried to phone Messrs. Fork and Sully. They were engaged.

Mrs S. had just returned from shopping when, with heavy heart, I let myself in the front door.

'Have a nice trip?' she asked, humming to herself as she unpacked some tasty-looking goodies.

'Fine, just fine,' I said. 'It only cost me about a hundred thousand quid.'

'You'd have been better off with a package.' said Mrs S.

I could see that she was not really interested in my troubles. She bustled around, putting the best tea things on the table and giving the milk jug a special rinse. I had a feeling that the balance of payments was going to be in the red again next month.

'What gives?' I asked. 'Having a party?'

'I'm expecting a visitor,' said Mrs S.

'Not the rabbi again?'

'Freddy,' she said, casually.

'I didn't know Freddy lived in Fulham?'

'He doesn't. But he promised to look in on the way home.'

'I see.'

Mrs S. was a fine-looking woman but of an age when a kind word, spoken in jest and with no great sincerity, could easily turn her head. I didn't like the idea of some old roue (that's a word I picked up in Jersey) leading her up the garden path.

'He's really quite interesting and ever so helpful,' said Mrs S. 'I may have misjudged him.'

'I expect his wife doesn't understand him, either,' I said, letting the bile of the blitzen krieg get the better of me.

'He's not married,' said Mrs S.

'Really?'

'No. He has to cook all his own meals.'

Except, I was tempted to say, the little snacks he picks up now and again at Fulham. Snacks, I might add, that were not previously available to fee-paying residents.

At half past five, the chimes of the front-door bell announced the arrival of the fatted calf.

'I'll go!' said Mrs S. excitedly, giving her hair a quick pat into place.

'Hullo, dear lady!' I heard the old roue warble as the front door was almost wrenched off its hinges. 'And how are we today?'

'All the better for seeing you,' replied the shameless old boot. 'Come in, the kettle's on.'

Freddy was surprised to see me in the kitchen, having a quick nibble at the shrimp vol au vonts.

'Hullo, dear boy,' he said, extending his hand. 'How nice to see you. Good holiday?'

'So, so,' I said, playing it close to my chest. 'I've been worrying over the trade figures.'

'And so you should, dear boy, and so you should. Frightful, absolutely appalling. But what can you expect from a government of economic neanderthals?'

He smiled at Mrs S. who was fiddling with a packet of paper serviettes. I noticed that the table had been set for only two.

'Freddy and I were just going to enjoy a quiet cup of tea,' said Mrs S. 'You can join us, if you like. You don't have to go.'

Something about the look on Freddy's face told me that a

discussion about the economic policies of a neanderthal government was the last thing he wanted at the end of a busy day. I made an excuse.

'I won't, if you don't mind. I'm feeling a bit shattered after the flight.'

'Jet lag,' said Freddy. 'You lay down and put your feet up for a while. Let your soul catch up with you.'

He smiled at Mrs S. as she poured him a cup of tea. I noticed that she was using the strainer, something she had not done before.

'I'll give you a ring tomorrow,' I said. 'We can discuss the trade figures then.'

'Righty-o, old boy.'

I trudged wearily upstairs and threw myself on the bed. What's a hundred grand, I asked myself, when you're a millionaire? The fact was, however, that with a hundred thousand quid now very definitely at risk in the books of Messrs. Fork and Sully I was not a millionaire. Moreover, I was a bit worried about my dealings on the foreign exchange market. Suppose Barry had put me into the German mark? Suppose Siggy had bought sixty eight contracts in pickled herrings? Suppose that Miss Abergombe was even now, as I put my feet up to recharge my batteries and keep a firm hold on my sanity, climbing over the Berlin wall, pursued by Villi clutching a suitcase full of fifty-pound notes?

I fell into a troubled sleep. Not surprisingly, I awoke with a muzzy head and a throat like an eagle's armpit. The headache I blamed on the trauma of being an active player in the capital markets; the thirst on the fact that alcohol leaves you dehydrated. I didn't want to disturb the cosy little tea party downstairs so I decided to dine out at the pizzeria in the High Street. There was no sign of life in the parlour, anyway, so I guessed the landlady and her gentleman caller must have gone out, too.

Surprise, surprise, but whom should I meet as I was walking past the Hospital for Nervous Diseases but my old mate Frankie! Frank, whose fare I had paid to Australia. Who had gone to Australia – or so I thought.

'Frankie!' I cried. 'I thought you were down under?'

'Just back on business,' said Frank, his vocal chords strangled by red gum and sheep dip. 'A conference, actually.'

I couldn't imagine Frank taking part in a conference but Australia has a strange effect on some people.

'Come and have a bite to eat,' I said. 'Tell me about it.'

To make him feel more at home, we took a cab to Earl's Court and managed to get a table at a little Paki joint that specialised in curried steak and chips, with an egg on top.

'So, what sort of business brings you to London to attend a conference?' I asked, trying to forget the £1,000 that had helped my old mate on the way to fortune.

'I'm a PR man,' he said.

'PR?'

'Public relations. You know, you tell people to drink bunyip juice because it's good for the skin and they all go out and buy it. Part of the marketing mix, really.'

'But you don't know anything about public relations!'

'You don't have to know anything to be a PR man,' said Frank, downing his second stubby of Swan lager. 'You just need a fork and a pair of green wellies.'

'What do you need those for?'

'To spread the bullshit,' said Frank.

'What about the Trade Descriptions Act? Or don't you have one of those in Australia?'

'No time to worry about things like that, sport. My job is to sell the product. Caveat emptor. Let the buyer beware.'

'Sounds a bit like stockbroking,' I said, wondering if the chef had been on a training course in Wagga Wagga.

'Too right,' Frank agreed. 'If some joker wants to buy a share, you don't tell him it's a dud, do you – unless you've been out in the sun too long.'

'But, surely, there must be more to PR than that? What about all this stuff called "improving the corporate image"?'

'That's bullshit, for a start,' said Frank. 'Suppose you've got this dodgy outfit pumping cyanide into the harbour? How you gonna improve its image – unless the cyanide kills all the sharks? The only way to make 'em respectable is to put all the waste in barrels and dump it out of sight in the bush. That's what PR is all about, old sport – making sure the public doesn't figure out what you're really doing.'

Old Frank had certainly pulled himself up by the bootstraps since he left the Old Country and settled Down Under.

'How did you manage to get into PR?' I asked. 'When you left here you were' – I had to stop myself saying skint and had to borrow £1,000 – 'not sure what you planned to do.'

'Great place, Australia,' said Frank. 'They give you a go. I was tossing up whether to take a job driving old age pensioners around this place called Surfers Paradise or selling tumble driers to Vietnam refugees when this joker at the job centre said, "If you can sell, why not go into PR? Pays a lot more than tumble driers and, in PR, they like the Poms. Gives the product a bit of class".

'Funny thing,' continued Frank, 'but they used to hate the Poms. Whinging Poms, they said. Complain about everything. Now they've got all these other poofters to take it out on' – he eyed the waiter – 'you know, so-called political refugees from Asia and the like. "Let me in or I'll be forced to live a life of poverty among my fellow countrymen".'

I hoped Frank wasn't turning into a racist. I had heard that Australia used to have a White Australia policy – which meant that, as long as you were white, you could get in and have meat three times a day. They've dropped all that now, though. Now, you can be any colour under the sun, so long as you can speak Greek and drink six schooners before lunch.

'What do you do besides selling shark repellent and attending conferences in London?' I asked.

'Oh, we've got a whole string of clients. Mainly retail, but some in agriculture, food processing, mining . . . '

He paused and glanced quickly around the tables at our fellow diners. For a moment, he looked like the shifty old Frank I had known in days gone by.

'As a matter of fact,' he said, lowering his voice, 'I could have a bit of news for you on the mining front one of these days.'

'But I'm not in the mining business.'

'No, but you're in the investment business, aren't you? Or

have you blown all that money yet?'

'I've still got some left,' I said, 'but investment seems to be a fairly risky business.'

'Yeah, well, keep a bit handy,' said Frank, pausing while the Paki cleared the plates away. 'One of our clients – a mining company – has got a couple of leases way out the back of Wop Wop – you know, beyond the black stump. I'm not on the account myself but one of the directors came in the other day and by the look on his face . . . ' He winked. 'Well, they're not spending all day and every day up there among the flies and mossies for nothing, are they? In fact,' he added, dropping his voice even lower, 'I bought a few shares on the strength of it myself. You know, just a little insurance policy in case they forget to tell Frank baby. Not a word, mind. They're pretty hot on inside information these days. In the States you can even go to jail – if they catch you.'

I had to admire the speed with which Frank had acquired his knowledge of the PR business, as well as of the mining and securities industries. It had taken me six months and half a million quid to learn as much as he had picked up in half the time in a PR outfit.

'Tell you what,' he said, 'why not take a little trip out there yourself and make a few enquiries. Just nosey around for a bit, see what you can find out. With your sort of backing, you could clean up a fortune.'

Well, the thought of going to Australia and leaving Mrs S. with all that cash under the bed and Freddy popping in and out for cups of tea aroused a conflict of interest, as Freddy was fond of saying. But I had never been to Australia and if Frank had done so well there, as he obviously had, there was a chance for me. Besides, here was an opportunity for me to back my own hunches, based on my own researches, without any help at all from my professional advisers. The early bird catches the worm, I reminded myself.

'Get yourself a visa,' said Frank. 'That'll give you six months to look around and size up the joint.'

'I'll go on one condition,' I said.

'What's that?'

'You come with me and show me around the mine.'

Frank pulled a face.

'Might be difficult,' he said. 'The boss will think it pretty damn suspicious if I suddenly go walkabout.'

'But if it turns out to be a gusher you'll be home and dry,' I said.

'This is a mine, not an oil well,' said Frank.

But I could see what he was thinking. Old Frank could never resist temptation, which is why he was in Australia in the first place. You could almost hear the grey matter ticking over.

'I guess I'm due for a couple of weeks' hol., anyway,' he said. 'But it won't be cheap, going right up north.'

'Don't worry about that,' I said. 'I'll bring my cheque book.'

'Okay, sport, you're on,' said Frank, leaning across the table and shaking my hand. 'Just give me a chance to get back out there and arrange a spot of leave and I'll meet you in Sydney.'

'Under the shade of a coolibah tree, cobber.'

I couldn't help noticing that at these words, which obviously meant a lot to Australians far from home, the whole restaurant looked up and in our direction. I wondered if they thought I was just another Pommy bastard taking the mickey out of a bunch of colonials. But we got away all right and Frank took the Tube back to his hotel.

'Thanks for the curry,' he said as we parted. 'By the way, I haven't forgotten the thousand quid.'

Good bloke, Frank. Even if he did get the push from PR, there was always a job driving pensioners around Surfers Paradise.

10. A tactical retreat

Freddy was looking worried. I had never seen him look so worried. Usually, when he came to visit Mrs S., he seemed to be on top of the world. I don't know what Mrs S. put in his tea but the effect, as they used to say, was shattering.

'Have you got a moment, Sid?' he asked. 'In private.'

'Anything wrong?' I enquired, leading him upstairs to the bedroom.

'Plenty,' he replied. 'We're in dead trouble, old chum.'

Now, when somebody says 'we're' in trouble and calls you 'old chum' when you're no more than business acquaintances, you know he is trying to pin some of the blame on you. Redistribution of guilt, so to speak. Freddy sat down on the little two-seater settee I had bought to smarten up the bedroom and took out his silk hankie.

'You remember Northern Puds?' he asked.

'Of course.'

'You did rather well out of them, as I recall?'

'Not too bad. Better than some of my other investments,' I could not resist adding.

'Never mind the others,' said Freddy. 'We're in a fix and we've got to wriggle out of it somehow.'

I must say, at that moment, Freddy went down in my estimation. Wriggling out of things was not what I was entitled to expect of my financial adviser. He sounded more like a chief constable on a speeding charge.

'Wriggle out of what?' I asked.

'To put it bluntly, Sid, old son, a charge of insider dealing.'

He wiped his brow and looked at me pleadingly, like a whipped cur.

'You remember how, when we first met, Bernie told you that we had had lunch with the chairman of Northern Puds?'

'Yes.'

'Well, that was not strictly accurate. Bernie does know the chairman – as a matter of fact, it's his brother – but we had not actually had lunch with him for some time.'

'How did you know the shares were a good buy, then?'

'A hunch, old boy, a hunch. Bernie held one or two shares himself, of course. Kept a brotherly eye on them, sort of.'

'What's the panic, then?'

'The Exchange seems to think that brotherly love has exceeded the bounds of duty. They've unearthed all the dealings in the shares just prior to the bid – I won't bore you with the details now – and concluded that, seeing as how Bernie was the biggest trader, he must have had some inside information.'

'Well, I didn't have any, that's for sure,' I said. 'I had no idea that that Arab fellah would come along with a bid.'

'Neither had we; I can give you my absolute word on that,' said Freddy. 'It came as a complete shock. The trouble is that the Exchange may not believe us.'

'If they can't see the truth when it smacks them in the eye, they shouldn't be allowed to poke around in people's private affairs,' I said loftily.

'Absolutely, old boy, absolutely. But you know what they're like: just because somebody runs off with half a dozen bottles of Guinness, they think everybody has something to hide.'

'Well, I'm in the clear,' I said. 'I had never heard of the company before you mentioned it and I have certainly never met Bernie's brother.'

'That won't exactly get Bernie and me off the hook,' said Freddy. 'They'll want to know why Bernie sold you his shares.'

'Bernie sold me his shares? I don't understand.'

'Well, you wanted to buy Northern Puds and, to be honest, there were not too many about. Fortunately, Bernie had a few of his own, so he very generously allowed you to have them.'

'Poor old Bernie,' I said. 'He would have done better holding on to them.'

'Yes he would,' Freddy agreed. 'But there's no point in crying over spilt milk. The Exchange has already asked what we knew about the bid – which was nothing, of course – or why you suddenly bought. I'm afraid you're the chief suspect, old son, so you'll need a good story that doesn't implicate your financial adviser or your broker.'

'I see.'

'Good. In that case, if anybody from the DTI or the fraud squad comes sniffing around you can tell them it was just a stroke of luck – which it was – that put you into the stock a couple of days before the bid. You needn't say anything about our little lunch date at Brighton. Just forget the whole thing. It wouldn't do if the Exchange thought that one of its members had been planning a bit of a ramp. The council might have something to say about that.'

'It wouldn't do if members thought that one of their number had advised a client to buy shares in a Christmas pud factory run by his brother, you mean?'

'Quite, old boy. But you do see, don't you, that we mustn't give these hounds the slightest grounds for suspicion. Once they're on the scent, it's the devil's own job to shake them off. So, if you see the hunt coming up the drive, just tell 'em to piss off, if you'll pardon the expression.'

Well, poor old Freddy must have been rattled to use language like that. I had never heard him use any expletive before, except a very mild one which I have deleted. But now here he was, wiping his brow as though he had just eaten a curry in a sauna bath, and mouthing obscenities. I wondered whether he had been reading the Daily Smut on his frequent visits to Mrs S. The trouble with smut is that you don't realise it has corrupted you until it is too late. By then, you have probably ruined your chance of mixing with the right crowd.

'Leave it to me,' I said. 'I can wriggle as well as the next man. But, I must say, I think Bernie ought to have told me that my Christmas puds were his Christmas puds. I mean, a client ought to be able to trust his broker, oughtn't he?'

'Absolutely, old boy. And I can assure you it won't happen again. As a matter of fact, Bernie hasn't got any more shares, anyway. In mitigation, I can only say that he was trying to do his best for you. After all, you wanted the shares and the only person with any to sell was Bernie. So, in a way, he really put your interests before his own, if you follow.'

'I think I do.'

'Good. Then if the fraud squad gets in touch, just forget you ever went to Brighton. And not a word to Isobel – Mrs S. – eh?'

'She was at the lunch, too,' I reminded him.

'Yes, but fortunately she didn't buy any shares.'

'I suppose,' I said, as we went downstairs, 'that Bernie hasn't got any Euro Jaunts or Bongo bonds, by any chance?'

'Don't be like that, old boy. As I said, he hasn't got any shares now.'

We found Mrs S. in the kitchen merrily going about her culinary business. A jug of freshly-brewed coffee and Madeira cake miraculously appeared.

'You've got time for a little nibble?' said Jezabel, flashing Freddy one of her winning smiles.

She certainly was a fine-looking woman. These days, there was a positive bloom on her cheek. I think it was partly the relief of knowing that Mother had found a permanent resting place, weighed down with a block of marble, courtesy of Sid.

'Sid's off to Australia soon; did he tell you?' said Mrs S., cutting Freddy an extra large slice of cake.

'No, he didn't,' said Freddy, mildly surprised. 'Not emigrating permanently, I hope?'

'Just a business trip,' I said and, with a slight frown at Mrs S., added: 'It was supposed to have been a secret.'

'Sorry,' said Mrs S. 'I seem to have let the cat right out of the bag.'

'I'm glad you did, dear lady,' said Freddy, absent-mindedly stirring his coffee with the cake fork. 'Might it not – in view of our recent conversation, old boy – be a good idea if you were to take the next flight? And if not the next flight then the one after that, if you see what I mean.'

I did see and I also saw that, if I did a bunk, the finger of suspicion would point indelibly at me. An innocent man, found guilty by default, simply because he was not there to defend himself. But, I told myself, British justice did not work like that, especially where Australia was concerned. That bloke with the funny hat proved that.

'Have you got your visa?' asked Mrs S., knowing full well that I had stood in the queue at Australia House that very morning waiting to get my passport stamped.

'Just rearin' to go,' I said.

'Then I do recommend an early flight,' said Freddy, putting the emphasis on the word flight. I got the message.

'I'll give Qantas a ring straight away,' I said. 'They're bound to have a spare seat.'

'Good on you, sport,' said Freddy, lapsing into the common speech of the antipodes. 'I'm sure a couple of months down under will do you a power of good.'

At least it would give me a chance to use my Australian cheque book.

11. Lucky for some

Frank was at the airport to meet me. I had cabled him from Singapore that I was on the way, carefully avoiding any suggestion that I was anything more than a run-of-the-mill tourist.

'What is the purpose of your visit?' asked the front-row prop at the immigration desk, giving me the once-over as though I'd escaped from a tin of cat food.

'I've just come to spend a few dollars, if that's all right?'

'All right by me, sport. But, with this visa, make sure you're on the way home within six months.'

He handed my passport back and waved me through. I, a representative of the country that had put Australia on the map, was allowed to set foot on the native soil of dingoes and wallabies.

'Have a good trip?' asked Frank, grabbing my bag.

'Not bad,' I said. 'Sorry to give you such short notice. Did you manage to fix up a holiday?'

'I'm working on it,' said Frank.

'What are you doing here today?'

'Taking a sickie. Told 'em I was suffering from salmonella poisoning. Plenty of that out here in the heat.'

'That's nice to know.'

'Don't worry, it's a very short-lived strain. I'll be as right as rain tomorrow,' he added, with a wink.

We took a taxi from the airport to a place called Kings Cross. As far as I could make out, it was the residential district of Sydney. Hotels, bars, delicatessens, people; everywhere you looked the place was teeming with life. We stopped outside one of the larger hotels.

'This do you?' asked Frank. 'Or do you want somewhere smaller?'

'This'll do,' I said. 'Best to be anonymous.'

I paid the driver and stood there waiting for him to unload the bags. Apparently, Australian taxi drivers are allergic to heavy weights. Egalitarianism, I think they call it. He just pressed a button to open the boot and left Frank and me to unload everything on to the pavement – and shut the boot.

'You'll get used to it,' said Frank. 'Just remember that an Australian is as good as the Prime Minister of bloody Singapore and you'll be right, mate.'

He led the way into the hotel which, I must admit, was pretty posh for this part of the world. It had what some bloke on the plane called 'a veneer of civilisation'. Rubber plants, upholstered chairs, even ashtrays so you didn't have to stubb out your cigarette on the parquet floor. The bird at reception was pretty cute, too.

'A single room sir?' she enquired. 'With single or double bed?'

And this without a flicker of an eyelid!

'Single, thanks,' said Frank, before I'd even considered the matter. 'And we'll take it for a week, to start with.'

'In that case, you'll want a double-bed, surely?' asked the sheila, with a charming smile.

Frank was mightily embarrassed.

'When I say "we", I don't mean us, I mean him,' he explained. 'He's just out from the Old Country and I'm showing him around.'

'I beg your pardon,' said the sheila. 'Welcome to Australia, sir.'

'Thank you,' I said.

She pressed a bell and a flunky in colonial uniform appeared to take the bags. At least the hotels had got their people trained properly, even if the taxi firms hadn't.

'What was all that about?' I asked as we followed the bags up in the lift.

'I'll tell you later,' said Frank. 'But, take my advice: unless you want to go down with something a lot worse than salmonella, stay away from the birds up here. And don't bend over to pick up any nine-bob notes.'

The flunky deposited my bags on the floor and pulled back the cover on the bed.

'Will that be all, sir?' he asked, expectantly.

'That's fine,' said Frank. 'Thanks, sport.'

The flunkey retired.

'You don't tip people here, then?' I asked.

'Not if you can help it,' said Frank. 'Now, listen, I've booked you in here just to give you a taste of the real Australia. If you go down there,' he said, pointing out of the window towards the harbour, 'you'll come to Wooloomooloo and the Opera House. And if you go down there' – pointing out of the other window – 'you'll find Rose Bay and Elizabeth Bay and all the little coves where the convicts came ashore and clubbed the locals to death.'

'You seem to have picked up the history pretty quickly,' I said, with admiration. 'I suppose that's what comes from being a PR man. What's in the other direction?'

'Brothels, mainly,' said Frank. 'I didn't like to tell you while the flunkey was here but there are more red lights in the Cross than there are on a Russian convoy. More queers, too, than any place except San Francisco.'

'And you've booked me in for a week? Gee, thanks, pal.'

'You might as well see the sights,' said Frank. 'You don't have to dip the wick every five minutes. Besides, it will give you a chance to unwind. I won't be able to get off till next week.'

'What news from the mine?' I asked.

'Shaping up very nicely,' said Frank, dropping his voice as though the walls might have ears. 'Core samples looking good.'

'Well, the quicker we get up there, the better. What's the name of this outfit?'

'Innaminute Minerals,' he said. 'If they strike it rich, they plan to set up a new company with a new corporate image. That's where we come in.'

'What are the shares doing at the moment?'

'Holding pretty steady. You can watch them being traded on the Exchange here, if you like.'

'Really?'

I had never seen a share traded. When I went to the Stock Exchange gallery in London, they said I was too late. There was nothing left to see. Just some blokes throwing paper aeroplanes about who, it was explained, were options dealers. I wondered where the telly got all those pictures of people buying and selling.

'Why don't we have a bite to eat and then catch up with the price?' said Frank.

'Good idea.'

We decided not to eat at the hotel, which was full of American sailors and birds with nothing better to do, but at an Italian joint in Elizabeth Street.

'That's David Jones,' said Frank, as we walked past a huge department store. 'Wish I had a few shares in that.'

'Why not buy some, then?' I asked.

'Too slow,' said Frank. 'You'll come out on the right side in the long run, of course, but they lack the bounce of a mining house.'

Bit like ICI, I thought, or that other Aussie company, BHP.

The meal, my first in Australia, was a bonza nosh, as they say down under. Gazpacho, Vienna schnitzel with Spanish salad, accompanied by a riesling from the Hunter Valley (Frank's choice), and a strange-looking concoction called a pavlova. It didn't break the bank, either, as it would have done in London. I could see why Frank had blossomed under the southern skies, even if the pavlova did seem to be the natural habitat of a short-lived strain of salmonella.

Feeling pretty pleased with ourselves, we strolled down Castlereagh Street towards the Exchange.

The public gallery overlooked the trading floor, just as it had done in London for the two hundred years before I arrived. But here, in Sydney, the joint was really jumping.

'The mining boards are down there,' said Frank, sounding like a guide at a holiday camp in Clacton. 'Innaminute Minerals, see it?'

I saw it.

'Not much happening at the moment,' said Frank. 'Those little chalk marks on either side show how many buyers and sellers there are. About equal at the moment, I'd say.'

'Then why don't they cancel each other out?' I asked.

'They would do, if they could agree on a price,' said Frank.

Just as he spoke, a chalkie pulled down the board, rubbed

out all the buyers and left the sellers standing there like a spare priest at a wedding.

'That's not so good,' said Frank. 'I hope nothing has happened to depress the price.'

'Perhaps the buyers just got tired of waiting?'

'Could be,' Frank said. 'It's not my account, of course, but if it were I might put out a Press release to steady the nerves.'

'Wouldn't you need to inform the Exchange first? Price-sensitive information and all that.'

'Stuff the Exchange,' said Frank. 'The client comes first.'

Frank was as good as his word. The following day he went back to work, completely recovered, to put the interests of his clients first. The sickie is apparently an Australian institution, on a par with grandmothers' funerals in the U.K. It's a much better idea, really, because you've only got two grandmothers (give or take a divorce or two) but you can go on having sickies, year in, year out. And, in a hot climate, there's no end of diseases to ring the changes with.

While Frank was working and, hopefully, getting what info he could from the guy on the mining account, I amused myself by exploring Sydney. Great place, even if it was the Aids capital of the South Pacific. When the first fleet arrived, it was inhabited by no more than a handful of aborigines. Once they had been driven away, the property speculators got to work. That's why, in the space of two hundred years, you've got acres and acres of concrete all over the place.

Mind you, there's a fair bit of water in between. I spent a whole day crossing the harbour on the various ferries and having the odd milk shake to pass the time. I even dipped my toes in the Pacific at a place called Manly. They've got two beaches there; one for macho types who don't mind being eaten by sharks, the other for old women and kids who feel safer behind a net. I waited till the surf was pretty low, then went into the water with the sharks. I figured that a shark would have to be pretty hungry to pick on me, a scrawny Pom, when there were blokes there with about twenty stone of muscle on them. But, I must say, thinking about the sharks took my mind off the Stock Exchange, all right.

142

On the Friday, just before I was due to meet Frank for the journey north to the mine, I sneaked back to the Exchange and took up my position in the public gallery. Innaminute Minerals were still there and so were the sellers. One or two buyers had even returned, to judge by the chalk marks.

There were some right-looking jokers in the gallery, too. Straight from the bush, if you ask me, with their short pants and blue singlets. Not quite the sort of punter you'd expect to find in London. But, as I kept reminding myself, this wasn't London and Australians were not British. They did things differently here. One guy even had a portable telephone that every so often he spoke into. I sort of edged closer to hear what he was saying.

'Jesus!' I heard him mutter. 'They've just pulled the plug on Meekatharra. Did you get rid of them okay? Right, we'll come back in again at 59. Let 'em drift for a while. What do you think of Woodside? No? Okay, I'm gonna call it a week, anyway. See yer at the polo.'

He put the telephone away and cast a parting scowl at the mining boards.

'They're not going to do much more today, anyhow,' he said. 'Too hot to get excited.'

'It's very cool in here,' I said, acknowledging the air-conditioning. 'It's very hot outside, though.'

'How long you been out from the Old Country, sport?' he asked.

'About three days,' I confessed.

'You wait till it gets really hot,' he warned. 'The Poms die off faster than Nips at Nagasaki.'

That was an Australian expression I had not come across before. I wondered if it was meant to be an insult but the joker seemed friendly enough.

'I suppose,' I said, 'you don't happen to know a broker who could buy me a few shares?'

'Listen, sport, the whole bloody building is full of 'em, all trying to make a dollar or two. Just look at the names at the foot of the lift shaft and take your pick.'

'I couldn't help overhearing your own conversation. Perhaps you could introduce me to your own broker?'

'Sure,' he said, 'although I don't see why I should help the bastard. He never puts any business my way.'

He pulled out the portable telephone and dialled a number.

'Al? Desmond. I got a Pom here looking for a broker. You interested?'

Desmond eyed me up and down, as though trying to gauge the width of my wallet. But, in my lightweight suit, nothing showed, at least, nothing of a financial nature.

'Okay, I'll send him round. Forget Meekatharra, by the way. I'll think about it over the weekend.'

Desmond jerked his head towards the exit.

'Okay. He'll give you a go. Follow me and I'll show you his office.'

'Is he . . . er . . . respectable?' I asked, hoping not to offend my colonial friend.

'Listen, sport, we don't go in for respectability out here. Brokers come in two sorts: those who stay put and those who run off with your money. So far, mine hasn't run off. That's about all I can say for him.'

'Mind you,' he added, as we went down in the lift, 'they still go a bundle for respectability in the bush. You been to the bush yet?'

'No, but . . . ' – I almost said, we're leaving tomorrow to check out a mine but stopped myself just in time – 'I hope to soon.'

'Take my advice, then. Get yourself a can of fly spray and a big hat and leave that poofter suit down here in the closet. Otherwise, you won't come back in one piece.'

We stepped out into the sunlight and walked down the street. I don't know if it was the heat or the thought that this was the land where the common man, i.e., Frank and me, could make a go of it but something in the air made me feel real good. We stopped outside a building that had obviously been put up by convict labour. Desmond jerked his thumb towards the door.

'Third floor, first on the left, ask for Al,' he said. 'He'll fix you up.'

'Thanks, cobber,' I said, extending my hand.

'My pleasure,' said Desmond. 'Mind you, I don't often go

out of my way to help a Pom but, there again, you don't often find a Pom in the public gallery. Good luck to you, old chap.'

I found Al sitting at his desk behind a huge pile of paper. Either the computer had run amok or his secretary had walked out on him. He was a little guy with a black moustache. Foreign, I thought. Definitely not the type to play polo on Sunday; more likely to be found in the saddling enclosure with a hypodermic in his hand.

'What can I do for you?' he asked, pointing to a chair.

'I was wondering if you could buy me a few shares?'

'You got any money?'

'I wouldn't be asking you to buy shares if I hadn't,' I replied.

'You'd be surprised what some jokers ask,' said Al. 'I could buy the whole flaming list and end up selling it again because the client thought he didn't need any money. What d'you want to buy?'

I hesitated. I wished to convey to Al, in the kindest manner possible, that I did not want half of Sydney to know that the Poms were buying up mineral rights.

'Okay. I don't mind hanging around like a fart in a phone box while you make up your mind whether to tell me,' said Al.

'It's a little company, up north,' I said hurriedly.

'They're all little companies up north. The big ones are down south, in Melbourne.'

'I meant, it's drilling up north.'

I could sense that Al was beginning to wish he had a needle handy.

'You got a broker in Pommy land?' he asked.

'I have several,' I said, hoping to restore my credibility. 'One for shares, one for commodities and one for foreign exchange.'

Al sat up and began to take notice.

'You're into commodities? And you've still got some money left?'

'As far as I know, I have.'

'You must have God on your side, sport. I'd give him a quick ring to check, if I were you.'

Al pulled one of the papers from the pile and began to scribble on it.

'Nobody out here makes money on commodities,' he said, 'even on the physicals. Farmers going broke every hour of the day.'

'It's pretty tough being a farmer, even in Europe,' I said.

'Europe!' snorted Al. 'You bloody Poms can count yourself lucky that I'm a stockbroker and not a member of the Tariff Board. Otherwise you'd find a bloody great tariff on everything from that part of the world until you bought our beef and butter again.'

'I'm sorry you've had a raw deal,' I said.

'So am I, sport. Next time there's a bloody war in Europe, you can fight it yourselves.'

I could see that Al was getting a bit bolshie. I decided to change the subject before he started attacking the Queen.

'You ever heard of Innaminute Minerals?' I asked.

'I helped to float 'em,' said Al.

'From what I hear, they're turning in some interesting core samples.'

'They must have got the bloody rig working again,' said Al. 'You want me to buy some?'

'Just a few. But don't tell the world.'

'It'll have to go up on the board, old son. Nothing's a secret in this town for very long – unless it's a company going bust. Then you don't find out till it's too late. A little trick we learned from the Poms. How many do you want?'

'A hundred thousand?'

'I'll see what I can do.'

He pulled another paper from the pile and tossed it into the out tray. I took the hint.

'I know I can rely on your confidentiality,' I said pointedly.

'You can, sport. But can I rely on your bank balance?'

'I reckon so, cobber.'

'Good. Then see yourself out, if you don't mind. And watch out for those sheilas up at the Cross. Half of 'em are blokes.'

'You can trust me,' I said. 'Anyway, I'm off to the bush tomorrow.'

Hell! Now I've blown the gaff, I thought. I must learn to watch my tongue. But if Al had cottoned on he let it pass.

146

I walked back along the quay and past the Opera House, which has replaced kangaroos on all the picture postcards. They reckon the bloke who built it couldn't add up. No sooner had he put down the first plank than some joker told him to add a couple of noughts to the bill. A bit like the Common Agricultural Policy that Al was on about, I thought. I decided that when I came back from the bush I would buy a ticket and maybe absorb a spot of culture. Funny, but in the Old Country I never felt like going to Covent Garden. Price of the seats put me off, I reckon.

Frank was waiting at the hotel when I arrived. He was sitting at a dinky little wrought-iron table in the foyer, drinking a cup of coffee. A couple of birds at the next table, with eye-lashes as long as bootlaces, were giving him a visual once-over. They smiled at me as I joined him.

'Listen,' he said. 'On second thoughts, you had better come and stay with me. The Cross is no place for a Pom with a lot of dough on a Friday night.'

'What's so special about Friday?' I asked.

'Pay day. And with the Americans in town it could get pretty rough. I've taken the liberty of booking you out – so pick up your bag and we'll go.'

To be honest, I thought it was a bit of a liberty, especially as I was just beginning to feel at home. But Frank obviously knew the joint better than I did and was only thinking of my wallet.

'Have I got time for a drink first?' I asked.

'Just a quick one, then.'

The two birds looked our way hopefully.

The waiter brought a capuccino which is something they used to serve in London when I was a kid. You don't see much of it now. Been driven out by the brewers, I suppose. I downed it as quickly as possible and prepared to leave. As we were passing the birds' table, one of them looked up and said:

'Hi, handsome! Like a naughty?'

'No, thanks,' said Frank. 'Nor anything that goes with it.'

'What's a naughty?' I asked as we walked on.

'Their product,' said Frank, lapsing into marketing jargon.

I glanced back at the two sheilas but they had lost interest and were inspecting their eyelashes in a mirror.

Frank's house (an apartment, really) was on the other side of the harbour so we took the ferry to Cremorne and struggled off with my bags. The taxi driver was most helpful, as usual.

'Where exactly is this mine?' I asked as we sat on the balcony after dinner. 'Is it far?'

'Everything in Australia is a long way,' said Frank. 'But how do you fancy North Queensland?'

'North Queensland? Crocodile country?'

'Yeah. But you won't see many crocs where we're going. We'll take the plane to Townsville, then the train to Charters Towers.'

'And then what?'

'I'm not sure,' said Frank. 'We'll see when we get there.'

'But you know where the mine is?'

'Not exactly. But we'll find it easily enough.'

As I recall, North Queensland is a fairly big place. I remember reading about these blokes who went out for a beer and never came back. Eventually, their bones were found, stripped bare by white ants and didgeridoos.

'Suppose we get lost?' I said.

'We'll ask somebody the way.'

I spent a restless night, wondering whether it might not be safer to stay at the Cross.

We stopped at Brisbane on the way up, the capital city of the Sunshine State, no less. It was bloody hot, too. No wonder Frank had told me to leave my vest in Sydney. That's the strange thing about Australia. The further north you go, the hotter – not colder – it gets. (The water goes down the plughole the wrong way, too, although I didn't make a point of studying it.) I had heard quite a lot about Queensland from this joker on the beach at Manly. Apparently, it's run by a wowser named Joe who won't give anyone else a look in. At first I thought he meant that the State was run by kangaroos. But I have since learned that there is a difference between a joe (premier) and a joey (infant marsupial). At Brisbane, there was no sign of either.

'We haven't started yet,' said Frank, with the confidence of a seasoned traveller. 'It's about eight hundred miles from here to

Townsville, then a bit more.'

At least they served lunch on the plane: seafood platter with a choice of wine. The Murrumbidgee sounded a bit like a species of gnat so I chose the Barossa. I was just getting the flavour when we landed at Townsville. Well, if Brisbane was hot, this was Hell warmed up. The heat came not only from above but seeped up through the tarmac. I could see why Poms took one gulp and got straight back on the plane to go home again. The tropics can be a bit of a shock if you've been brought up on English summers.

As we staggered towards the airport terminal, a couple of jets – military types, not civilian – screamed overhead.

'Air Force base in Townsville,' explained Frank. 'Front line of defence against the yellow hordes.'

'I thought Australia was on good terms with Asia now?'

'Now, yes. But there are blokes around here who can remember Pearl Harbour. They're not taking chances.'

We decided to stay in Townsville for the weekend, or what was left of it, and take the train to Charters Towers on Monday morning. Our hotel looked as if it might have been thrown overboard by Captain Cook who ran aground in these parts, you know. A wooden balcony adorned the entire length of the first floor. It could have been painted once although I wouldn't swear to it. A pair of Abos squatted in the shade by the front door.

'We'll go down to the bar and see if we can pick up some information,' said Frank, after we had recovered from the journey. 'This place is the end of the line for trains from the outback. Everything is funnelled through here.'

Frank was right about it being the end of the line. But I felt he was pushing his luck if he expected to pick up any inside information. As far as I could see, the bar was a dead loss. For a start, no sheilas. Just a couple of blokes screwed to their seats. I didn't fancy waltzing up to them and asking what they knew about Innaminute. They might have unscrewed themselves. Frank tried the indirect approach.

'Nobody in from the bush tonight?' he asked the barman.

'Why? You expecting somebody?'

'No, just wondering how they were getting on at the mine.'

'The Isa, you mean?'

'No, Innaminute.'

'Never heard of it,' the barman said, and moved away to serve the fixtures.

Frank drained his glass and belched, as per the local custom.

'Let's go and find somewhere to eat,' he said.

I don't mind telling you that I wasn't sorry to leave Townsville. For all its strategic importance (a phrase I picked up from the radio) it remined me of one of those South Sea islands where the natives sleep under palm trees all day long and just get up for the beer. Sure, the trains come in from the west and the abattoirs are kept pretty busy with cattle from the stations. You get quite a lot of visitors there, too, especially from Asia. And, of course, all the time these RAAF jets are flying about the place, just to remind you that the little yellow and brown fellahs might not be tourists but spies planning an invasion. Frank told me how the Nips (I discovered that meant Japanese) had caught 'em all napping in Darwin during the war and how for years afterwards the harbour was filled with sunken ships. But, even with history all around us, I found it hard to stay awake.

First thing on Monday, we trundled down to the station to catch the train to Charters Towers. Pleasant surprise Number One: the train was comfortable and air-conditioned. Surprise Number Two: it left on time. I wondered afterwards whether this might not have something to do with the Japanese influence. We zigzagged through a range of scrub-covered hills and before long were out on the plain. Some joker told me that the railway had its own signature tune – I'll walk beside you – which the guard played whenever the track had been washed away. But I didn't believe him. Soon, the scrub gave way to a collection of shacks with tin roofs.

'Grab your bag,' said Frank. 'This is it.'

Well, if there had been a wild goose flying over the town at that particular moment I would not have been at all surprised. For the first time since arriving in Australia a week earlier, I wished I was back at Balls Bros. in the City. Even Townsville would have been preferable to Charters Towers.

'You wouldn't think this place had a stock exchange at one time, would you?' said Frank, as the taxi drove us down the main street in search of accommodation.

'That's right,' the driver chimed in. 'Closed down about a hundred years ago, when the gold ran out.'

'That's a hopeful sign,' I said to Frank, although we had agreed not to speak publicly about the purpose of our visit.

'What's a pair of Poms doing so far from home?' the driver asked.

'Just passing through,' said Frank.

'S'pose you wouldn't be connected with that little old rig, drilling away out there in the bush, by any chance?'

'Oh, is somebody drilling for oil?' asked Frank, innocently.

'Not oil, just copper. I'll run you out there, if you like.'

'I don't suppose it would do any harm to have a look,' I said, exchanging a quick glance with Frank. 'But we're really here on holiday, aren't we, old son?'

'Too right,' said Frank.

'Well, if you feel like taking a ride, just let me know.'

He nosed the taxi into the forecourt of a Captain Cook, Mark II, hotel.

'There you are, sports. That'll be three dollars. Cost you a bit more to go to the rig but, seeing as how you're on holiday, I'll give you a discount.'

'That's very kind of you,' I said, as Frank paid the fare. 'At least, it would give us something to do.'

'Help to pass the time,' Frank agreed.

The drive handed me a card with his name and telephone number on it.

'Just give me a ring and I'll be round here before you can say Stuff Bjelke-Petersen.'

'By the way,' said Frank, 'what's the name of this drilling outfit?'

'One a minute, we call it. A ramp, if you ask me. But someone's making money out of it.'

Frank nodded sagely.

'I wonder why they call it one-a-minute?' I asked as we

151

unpacked in the double room that the hotel had managed to find for us. 'Surely, they don't find minerals at the rate of one a minute?'

'No,' said Frank. 'Just investors.'

He seemed a bit uptight. At first, I thought it might have been over the three dollars he had coughed up for the taxi. But, as a responsible PR man, he was obviously concerned about his client's image. If the nickname stuck, he and his mates would have their work cut out re-establishing what he called 'an acceptable corporate identity'. Although it was not his account, I suspected that he intended to raise the matter with the powers that be when we got back to Sydney.

By lunchtime, I was getting used to life in the outback. It wasn't too bad, all things considered. The pub wasn't Balls Bros., by any means, but it put on a pretty good spread and seemed to have a direct line to the brewery. Truckies, bank clerks, shopkeepers, corrugated tin salesmen, all crammed into the bar, yacking nineteen to the dozen. I had been told they spoke real slow in Queensland but I could hardly keep up with this lot. I wondered if any of the drillers from the rig were there but, if they were, they didn't let on. As Frank had explained, it was a tight hole.

Our presence had already created a stir. I don't think many Poms ventured this far from the coast, certainly not without their vests. One bloke, in particular, kept edging closer as though trying to hear what we were saying. But, as I have already indicated, Frank and I were maintaining a tight hole policy, too. Only once did I mention my stockbroker in London and that was when the bloke had gone for a refill.

The following morning I phoned the taxi driver and told him to set the day aside for us. He was round at the hotel in no time, just as he had promised.

'I thought we might have a look at the countryside,' I said casually, as we piled into the back.

'Oh, yeah? Which bit do you want to have a look at first? The bit with the mulga or the bit with the diamonds?'

'Are there diamonds here, too?' I asked.

'Plenty, out at the rig.'

'Really?'

'Yeah, the bit's covered with 'em. Helps to cut through the rock.'

Sid, I said to myself, you fell for that one hook, line and sinker. And you don't even know what the mulga is.

'I'll settle for the diamonds,' I said. 'One or two might have worked their way loose.'

I don't know if you've ever driven over dirt roads that have been baked in the sun, then turned into mud by tropical storms, only to be churned up and baked hard again, but they do not compare with the M1. Before we had gone a couple of miles, I was feeling a bit groggy.

'Knocks hell out of the cars,' said Blue. 'Need a new one every twelve months or so.'

'I'll take your word for it. But you can slow down, if you like. We're in no hurry.'

'Jeez!' cried Blue. 'You can tell you've never been to the bush before. If you slow down, it's a bloody sight worse. I was taking it easy so you could get a look at the mulga. But, if you've seen enough, I'll step on the gas.'

Amazing, really! As soon as he put his foot down, we stopped bouncing around. It was just like being in a hovercraft on the Solent. And, by process of elimination, I figured that the mulga must be the bush itself. There was nothing else to see.

We sped on, down a road as straight as a die. Once, we passed a collection of humpies that Blue said was an Abo settlement. But the only sign of life was the swirling cloud of red dust behind us.

'What happens when we slow down?' I asked. 'Does the dust overtake us?'

'It sure does,' said Blue. 'That's when you get the full flavour of the bush.'

About ten miles down the road, we began to reduce speed.

'If you look out to the left, you'll see the rig,' said Blue. 'Do you want a guided tour?'

'Is that possible?' asked Frank. 'I'd heard it was a tight hole.'

'So it is. But these jokers wouldn't know an ore body from a whore's bodice. They're only drilling the hole.'

153

Our guide pulled off the road and drew to a halt by the side of the rig. We waited for the dust to settle, then opened the door and got out. A bloke with a belly the size of an elephant glanced in our direction.

'G'day, Kit!' cried Blue, shouting to make himself heard over the noise of the diesel engine.

Kit, whose khaki shorts, blue vest and brown hat were all liberally smeared with grease, waved a greeting.

'G'day, Blue! More tourists?'

'Couple of Poms, looking for something to write home about.'

'Well, you won't find much out here, except the biggest pile of stubbies this side of Humpty Doo.'

He swiped at half a dozen flies that were buzzing around his hat. They retreated a couple of feet, then flew back again.

'I reckon you'll be wanting to know if we've struck gold yet,' he said. 'The answer is no and, even if we had, we wouldn't know the grade until the core had been assayed.'

'I thought you were drilling for copper?' said Frank.

'Copper, eh? And I thought you were a couple of tourists?'

'We are,' I said quickly, hoping to retrieve Frank's technical blunder. 'I'm fresh out from the Old Country.'

'And just couldn't wait to get a look at our little rig?' said Kit. 'Well, by rights I should tell you to clear off before I put a bullet up your arse. But we don't get many visitors out here, except the bloody Abos who come and stare at us all day.' He took another vicious swipe at the flies. 'If you were thinking of pegging any claims, I can tell you not to bother, sport. We've got the whole place sewn up for miles around.'

'You've got it all wrong!' cried Frank. 'We're not in the mining business. I'm in marketing and Sid here is . . . er . . . sort of connected with finance.'

'You're not one of these Pommy fund managers, come out here to stock up the larder?'

'I don't know what a fund manager is,' I replied, truthfully. Blue chuckled.

'I knew a Pommy fund manager once,' he said. 'Wanted to buy Poseidon. I sold him all mine – at two eighty. I heard he was sacked soon afterwards.'

'I'm self-employed,' I said.

I had a nasty feeling that Frank and I were out of our depth. Here, among the flies and the stubbies, were two experts, even though one of them couldn't recognise an ore body when he saw it.

Kit offered a grubby hand.

'Nice meeting you, sport,' he said. 'Give my regards to the Old Country. And say hullo to Chuck and Di next time you see them.'

'Will do. With pleasure.'

'See you, Blue,' said Kit and, with a final swipe at the flies, went back to count the diamonds.

'What do you want to look at now?' asked Blue as we got back into the taxi. 'The mulga or the Abo camp?'

'Why don't we just look into a nice, cold glass of beer?' said Frank, coming up with the first sensible idea of the day.

I didn't want to say anything in front of Blue, who was obviously smarter than the average taxi driver, but I was thinking pretty hard as we sped back to town. Why, I asked myself, had I come all this way, spent a small fortune on fares and exposed myself to the dangers of heat stroke, sheilas and flies, just to look at a bit of machinery in the middle of bloody nowhere? Had I known how much information would be available on site, I could have called up Kit from the comfort of Kings Cross. But now here I was, in the bustling centre of the universe, where the stock exchange had closed a hundred years ago and Pommy fund managers were lucky to escape with a bullet up their arse.

'Thanks, Blue,' I sighed, handing over a wad of notes at the hotel. 'If we want you again, I'll give you a ring. Otherwise, have the rest of the day off on me.'

'Listen, sport,' growled Blue, 'I don't need charity, especially from a bloody Pom. There are enough bludgers in this town, anyway, without encouraging them.'

He peeled off half a dozen notes and stuffed them in his pocket. Then he returned the rest to me. I knew what it was like to be on the receiving end of charity.

'Come and have a beer, then?' I managed to say at last.

'I wouldn't say no to that.'

For a PR man, Frank was unnaturally quiet. I guessed he was wondering, too, what the hell we were doing in Charters Towers.

'Well, old son,' he said, as we sat down to lunch, 'if that was our mine, I'd say we were better off out of it.'

'But I thought you were supposed to be promoting it?'

'Yeah, well, you do a lot of funny things in public relations.'

'You're lucky, really, that it's not your account.'

Frank chewed his barbecued steak for half a minute and then said: 'I know! Why don't we have a look at a real mine?'

'A real mine?'

'Yeah. We could hire a plane and fly out to the Isa. We could be there and back in half a day.'

'And what good would that do?' I asked.

'It would keep us on the move, for a start.'

'So would a packet of figs. And they're a lot cheaper.'

'Yeah, but you don't want to start counting your pennies after coming all this way. The Isa mine is one of the seven wonders of the world.'

'I haven't seen the other six yet,' I reminded him.

'Fair go, mate. It's the chance of a lifetime.'

I swiftly calculated the odds of my visiting Mt Isa in future.

'Okay,' I said. 'Anything to get out of this place.'

'Good on you, sport,' said Frank, with renewed enthusiasm. 'I'll see if the flying doctor's going that way tomorrow.'

After lunch, while he was chasing up the owner of the local fly-a-Pom service, I put in a sneaky call to my broker in Sydney.

'Listen,' I said. 'You know those Innaminutes I told you to buy?'

'All yours,' said Al. 'Just in time, too. You must have had your ear pretty close to the ground there, I reckon.'

'What do you mean?'

'Price jumped five cents this morning. Word is the locals are buying. That's always a good sign.'

'But I was thinking of selling.'

'I'd hang on for a while yet, sport. They could build up a nice head of steam.'

'I don't want to lose any money.'

'You're doing all right, sport. I'll ditch 'em if they look like turning sour.'

The news put an entirely different complexion on my visit to the outback. When you're making money, even Charters Towers can seem quite attractive. In fact, I may have been over-hasty in my judgement. Rumour has it that, in the past, the place had three times as many women as men and was a regular watering point for blokes on the way out from the bush. One joker who had lost a leg fighting off a shark on the Barrier Reef even tried his luck there, they reckon. No sooner got off the train than five birds claiming to be nurses rushed up to examine his middle leg. But that was years ago. Now the birds have all got cars and just drive over the hill to the RAAF base when the heat and dust get them down. Not that I was interested in the sexual history of Charters Towers. But I wondered why the locals had started to buy into One a Minute.

You can see Mount Isa from about fifty miles because of all the smoke in the air. It comes from the big smelter at the mine, which goes in for lead and zinc and that sort of stuff. But once you've seen the chimney and sampled the steak and chips there's not much to do in the Isa. So, after lunch, we flew back to Charters Towers.

'I don't know about you,' said Frank, as we climbed out of the aircraft, 'but I think we should call the whole thing off. Let's go back to Sydney before you spend any more dough.'

'Suits me,' I said. 'I'll take in the Hanging Gardens of Babylon next year.'

I didn't like to tell Frank that, unbeknown to him, I was actually making money. Clearly, he had a guilty conscience about dragging me all this way to look at the mulga. I thought I'd let him suffer for a while.

We checked out in time to catch the evening train. Blue drove us to the station. He seemed sorry to see us go.

After an overnight stop at Townsville, we flew back to Sydney. The first thing I did was go and see Al, my antipodean broker.

'You certainly picked a winner there, sport,' he said, indicating the latest price on the screen. 'Last sale, 35 cents. Wish I'd bought some myself, now.'

'What's got into them?' I asked.

'The word from up north is that a couple of jokers from one of the big finance houses in London have been out to size up the joint.'

I was on the point of saying 'It's a wonder I didn't see them' when I remembered that our visit was supposed to be a secret. Instead, I said: 'Poms, you mean.'

'Yeah. Been spending money like water, hiring planes, flying all over the place. Now, you don't get Poms to splash out unless they're going to get something in return. So, those in the know have been piling into the stock. Look!' he exclaimed, jabbing a finger at the screen. 'Thirty eight cents! How much did you pay? Eleven? That's 27 cents a share profit – less commission, of course.'

'Maybe I ought to buy some more?' I said, nevertheless puzzled by the news and irritated by the fact that Al, who had been playing polo all weekend, seemed to know more about One a Minute than I did.

'Wouldn't do any harm,' he said. 'Even if they take a dip you'll average out all right.'

'Buy me another hundred thousand, then . . . no, make it two hundred thousand.'

'A quarter of a million is a nice round figure,' said Al.

'Okay, a quarter of a million.'

Al picked up the phone that connected him to his runner on the floor of the stock exchange.

'Buy 250,000 Innaminutes,' he barked. 'At best.'

He replaced the receiver.

'That should jolly them up a bit,' he said. 'You watch.'

Indeed, even as we watched the price on the screen edged higher: 41, 42, 45.

'Probably won't be able to get 'em all today,' said Al. 'But leave it with me. We won't chase 'em over the moon. By the way,' he added, 'you owe me eleven thousand dollars. Would you like to pay now, just to keep the record straight?'

Frank decided that, expedition over, he might as well go back to work. I moved back to the Cross. It seemed quite cosmopolitan after Charters Towers. I figured it wouldn't be long before word got out re the comings and goings up north and the shares took off – perhaps like that Tasminex outfit, some years ago. Frank decided he'd had enough – even if they were on the brink of a major mineral discovery – he sold out at 40. At least he made a profit.

They don't have a Daily Smut in Sydney. Instead, they have something called The Australian. Quite intellectual, all things considered. Anyway, I was reading it in the foyer after breakfast when I spotted this story about Abos in North Queensland. Well, having seen a real live Abo sitting outside the pub in Townsville, I was interested, of course. Apparently, to celebrate the two hundredth anniversary of all their land being taken away and their ancestors being hunted down and shot, the Queensland government was giving them a back a bit of scrub here and there. Not like the homelands in South Africa, where they put barbed wire around great chunks of the Veld to keep the boongs out of the way, but – according to The Australian – as 'a belated concession to the misdeeds of the past'. Now the bloke outside the pub in Townsville would have his own patch to sit on, if he wanted. Of course, the real Aussies – the convict classes who delivered the beer, published the newspapers, etc. – would still be allowed on to Abo territory. No passports or anything like that. Somebody said that Joe wouldn't approve but I don't know what he meant.

I had a quick squint at the share price (which was only yesterday's closing price, of course) and gave the paper to a couple of birds who looked as if they could do with a spot of intellectual nourishment. Then, at peace with the world, I walked down William Street to the city.

Al was in one hell of a panic when I arrived.

'Thank Christ you're here!' he cried. 'I tried the hotel but you'd already left. What are we going to do?'

'Do about what?' I asked, sensing further misdeeds.

'About these bloody Abos,' he said. 'Look at this.'

He flicked through the reports on the screen till he found a statement put out through the Stock Exchange by Innaminute Minerals. The gist of it was that a patch of mulga, the very same patch of mulga that Frank and I had just travelled three thousand miles to investigate and evaluate, had been handed over to the aborigines.

'What does that mean?' I asked, fearing the worst.

'What doesn't it mean?' Al growled, switching to the prices. 'Knocked hell out of the market, that's what. Just look at the volume. Like a flaming slaughterhouse.'

Indeed, the blood seemed to be flowing quite freely. After an early sale at 45, the price fell rapidly to 40, 35, 28. Even as we watched, somebody baled out at 20.

'What do you want to do?' asked Al. 'Get out or wait for the panic to stop?'

A decision was called for. I could see my fortune ebbing away. What would Bernie have done? I had never been in one of these ongoing situations before and for a moment I was paralysed. The next sale decided me.

'Sell!' I cried. 'Immediately!'

Al picked up the phone and frantically wound the bell.

'Sell 350,000 Innaminutes, now!' he screamed. 'At best.'

Well, I won't bore you with the hieroglyphics that suddenly appeared on the screen. But I can tell you that the entire attention of the Sydney Stock Exchange seemed to be focussed on our little patch of dirt outside Charters Towers. Sixteen, fifteen, eleven, ten.

'For Christ's sake!' muttered Al, frantically scratching his bum.

Nine, eight . . .

The telephone rang. Al listened.

'No takers,' he said. 'We've managed to offload a hundred thou. but that still leaves you with a quarter million.'

'Keep trying,' I said.

'Leave 'em on the board,' Al shouted down the phone.

He wiped his forehead and stared at the prices on the screen.

'Looks like you've caught a bit of a cold, old sport,' he said. 'How much of a cold?'

Al consulted his calculator.

'At the moment, excluding commission and provided they don't fall below eight, about a hundred grand.'

He looked at me closely.

'Not many blokes can afford to lose that sort of money,' he said, 'unless they're on pretty good terms with their bank manager.'

'Don't worry,' I said. 'I have several bank managers.'

By the time we had converted the loss into sterling, it didn't look so bad. But it would have looked a lot better if my friend in the PR business had never heard of Charters Towers.

I was pretty angry as I walked back up William Street. I didn't mind making a contribution to aboriginal land rights but I objected to subsidising a whole tribe. And what about these two blokes from London? They must have known something was in the wind. That's why they were there, calculating how much they stood to lose.

By the time I got to the top of the hill I felt like taking it out on one of these Aussie sheilas and giving her what for. Several were hanging about, pretending to be tourists. I sidled up to one with long, blonde hair and, ignoring all the advice given to travellers in foreign parts, said: 'Busy?'

'Never too busy to entertain a gentleman,' she said, taking my arm. 'You got plenty of money?'

'Enough,' I said, 'although not as much as I had this morning.'

The bird smiled. She was a well-built sheila with a touch of the farm about her. I could imagine her chopping wood out there in the bush and kicking the cow when it put its foot in the bucket.

As we were crossing the road, a sudden gust of wind – willi willies, they call them – roared up from the harbour and caught us amidships. I braced myself and clung to the bird.

'Jesus!' she cried hoarsely, wrenching herself free.

I noticed that her blonde wig had come adrift and was rolling down the street like a hedgehog in distress. The sheila galloped after it, revealing a very masculine turn of speed and an even more masculine short back and sides. What was it that Al had said about 'those sheilas up at the Cross'?

I turned quickly into the nearest shop and spent a fruitful five minutes browsing through Christian pamphlets until I reckoned it was safe to make a run for it.

Some joker once described Australia as a lucky country. I'd like to meet him one day. Take him to Charters Towers and show him the sights.

I phoned Frank from the hotel and told him I was going home. If this was the lucky country, I'd prefer to chance my arm in the old one.

12. Return of the Prodigal Pom

Freddy was almost as surprised to see me as I was to see him when I rang the bell at Mrs S.'s boarding establishment just off the Fulham Road. His jaw dropped, then rapidly hoisted itself again as he remembered his status as an officer and a gentleman.

'Sid, old boy!' he exclaimed. 'I didn't expect to see you for another month or so.'

'I'm allergic to sunshine,' I said.

'Australia not to your liking, then?'

'Oh, Australia's all right. Very moral society. Mind if I come in?'

'Sorry, old boy,' said Freddy, stepping aside somewhat reluctantly. 'I'll tell Isobel you're back.'

'Don't worry. I'll nip up to my room and unpack. I've got a little something for her.'

Freddy's jaw dropped once again and a note of embarrassment crept into his voice.

'Just hold on a tick, old boy,' he said. 'You see . . . well, how shall I put it?'

'Put what?'

Freddy shuffled his feet uncomfortably. I figured he was trying to tell me something. But the Poms, unlike the Aussies, never come straight out with it. As I waited, Mrs S. came down the stairs. She looked a little flustered.

'Mr Arbuthnot!' she gasped. 'I didn't expect you home so soon.'

I knew something was up because she hadn't called me Mr Arbuthnot since I was a month behind with the rent.

'A pleasant surprise for you,' I remarked.

'Yes, indeed,' said Freddy, although he did not exactly sound very pleased.

'Something wrong?' I asked.

'Wrong?' said Mrs S. 'No, of course not. What a silly thing to say.'

'That's all right, then. Now, if you'll give me time to unpack,

163

I'll show you what I picked up for you Down Under.'

I moved to make my way up the stairs. Mrs S. stepped swiftly in front of me.

'Well, you see, Sid,' she began, and it was then that I knew for sure that something was wrong.

'See what?' I prompted.

Mrs S. struggled for words.

'Well, the point is, old boy,' said Freddy, breaking the impasse, 'that your room – that is to say, the room you used to occupy – is temporarily out of commission, so to speak.'

'Out of commission?'

'Sort of . . . sub-let,' volunteered Mrs S.

'Sub-let? Who to?' I demanded.

Freddy lowered his eyes and looked a little shame-faced.

'To me, I'm afraid.'

I put down my case and stared at him.

'Now, don't get angry, Sid,' implored Mrs S., suddenly very emotional and feminine. 'It's only a temporary arrangement and if I'd have known you were coming back so soon I'd never have done it.'

'I'm afraid it's all my fault, old boy,' said Freddy. 'You see, I hadn't got anywhere to go and so Isobel – Mrs S. – took pity on me. But don't worry. I'll pack my bag immediately and depart. The client must always come first.'

'Now, wait a minute,' I said. 'Let's get this straight. I thought you had a big house in the country?'

'That's not strictly true, I'm afraid,' said Freddy. 'The fact is that I did live in a big house . . . but it wasn't mine, if you see what I mean. I'm only a half-commission man.'

'And what's that when it's at home?'

'It means I share the commission with Bernie on all the business I put his way.'

At that moment, the penny (or, to be more precise, several thousand pounds) dropped.

'So that means I've been supporting the pair of you?'

Freddy nodded.

'And, of course, when you went to Australia he had nothing to live on', said Mrs S. 'What was I to do?'

Well, since my visit to Kings Cross and being stuck on the plane next to some guy who raved on about the infidelities of the distaff side nothing much surprised me any more. I was no longer shocked by the vagaries of human nature. If poor old Freddy had been trying to impress his clients by saying he lived in a big house, he was doing no more than Frank or me when we put a million quid in each other's bank accounts. Nobody likes to admit they live in a hovel.

'Where will you go if you have to leave here?' I asked.

'I shall probably find somewhere,' said Freddy. 'There's always the Salvation Army.'

'You'll go to the doss house over my dead body!' cried Mrs S., suddenly very emotional again. 'And you'll not be turned out on to the streets at this time of night.'

I glanced at my watch. Half past six. Barely time for the cardboard boxes to come out under Charing Cross station.

'Why don't we have a cup of tea and work something out?' I said.

'An excellent idea!' replied Freddy. 'I was about to suggest it myself.'

So that's really how I came to leave Mrs S.'s establishment. It was agreed over tea and a slice of Fortnum and Mason Walnut Delight that Sid, world traveller and possessor of up to half a million quid, would book in at the Inn on the Park in an effort to reduce homelessness among needy members of the Stock Exchange. Even though I had paid a month's rent in advance, I couldn't chuck poor Freddy on to the mean streets of merry England.

'How did the investigation go, by the way?' I asked. 'Were you able to satisfy the Exchange?'

'To be absolutely honest, old boy, that's one of the reasons I have moved in here. Nobody expects to find a stockbroker in Fulham, even a half-commission man.'

'What about Bernie?' I asked.

'He is helping police with their enquiries, as they say.'

'That's why we thought it better if Freddy lay low here for a while,' said Mrs S., clearly relieved to explain the double occupancy. 'I'm sure it will all blow over.'

'Bound to,' said Freddy. 'After all, we've done nothing wrong.'

I finished my Walnut Delight and, opening my executive briefcase, took out the small parcel I had inadvertently forgotten to declare at the Customs.

'Here,' I said, handing it to my late landlady. 'A little prezzy.'

'What is it?'

'Open it and see.'

Mrs S. unwrapped the colourful David Jones paper bought especially for the purpose and laid it carefully to one side. I knew she would cherish that as much as the contraband. Then she opened the lid of the cardboard box and out popped the daintiest little opal that ever came out of Lightning Ridge.

'Oh, Sid!' she cried, flinging her arms around my neck and kissing me fondly on the cheek. 'What is it?'

'Unless I'm very much mistaken, it's a rather splendid opal,' said Freddy, taking the bauble and revolving it slowly to examine the fire. 'Magnificent! You'll be able to wear that with pride, my dear.'

He pinned it to her bosom and stood back to admire it.

'I've always fancied digging for opals myself,' he said. 'Much more exciting than digging for gold in the City.'

I was glad the prezzy had been so well received. I hoped Freddy wouldn't feel too cut up by the fact that I had brought nothing for him. But his eyes were glued firmly to Mrs S.'s bosom. A fine-looking woman, Mrs S., especially with an opal brooch.

'Well, I'll just nip up and get my belongings,' I said, making for the door.

'Don't worry, old boy,' said Freddy hastily. 'I'll go. I've packed everything of yours away ready, anyway.'

Before I could stop him, he was up the stairs three at a time. I was alone with Mrs S. I was sorry to be leaving. Now I knew how the Abos felt when they were turfed off their land by the convicts.

'What shall we do about the mattress?' said Mrs S., lowering her voice.

'The mattress?'

'The money,' said Mrs S. 'Do you want to call round and collect it?'

I thought rapidly as I could hear Freddy stumbling downstairs with the case.

'Leave it where it is for the moment,' I said. 'Nobody will find it there, will they?'

'Nobody except yours truly,' she smiled. 'But I really am sorry about this, Sid. I suppose that now you'll think I'm awful?'

'Here you are, old boy,' said Freddy. 'I think you'll find everything there. Shall I call a taxi?'

'Yes, please,' I said. 'One client and three bags for the Inn on the Park.'

The Inn on the Park is a cut above the joint I stayed at in Sydney, I can tell you. For a start, they don't have birds hanging around the foyer. Pretty classy, all told. I was beginning to wonder if they'd let me in. It was my executive luggage that saved me in the end, I guess.

But class costs money and a bloke with three brokers to support can't live in the lap of luxury for the rest of his life. So, first thing the following morning, I took the train to Penge to consult Brian, my accountant.

'How much do you reckon you lost down under, then?'

I told him, in dollars. He checked the exchange rate in the F.T. and fed the information into his personal computer.

'You're lucky the Australian dollar is so weak at the moment,' he said. 'If they'd still been living off the sheep's back, you'd be right up the creek.'

'I'm far enough up it already,' I replied.

We turned from foreign exchange to share prices and checked the residual value of my portfolio. ICI was holding up pretty well and so were the other blue chips. But Renaissance Properties had taken a real nosedive. Bongo 14 per cent redeemable bonds were a complete write-off.

'That leaves your commodity and foreign exchange positions to be evaluated,' said Brian. 'I'd have a quick check on those, if I were you. But, on the whole, you're not doing too badly. Still got about four hundred grand to play with.'

'But I had nearly a million six months ago!'

'That's the stock market for you, I'm afraid,' said Brian. 'Of course, everybody hopes their shares will go up. But very often they go down. It's a very risky business. You've got to be very lucky to make money on the Stock Exchange.'

'So it would seem.'

'Don't forget, every time you buy a share, it means that somebody has sold one. What you have to ask yourself is, why has he sold it?'

'To pay the gas bill, perhaps?'

'Or pass the buck?'

Well, I must admit, I had never thought of investment as a game of pass-the-parcel. According to the Daily Smut, shares were the grist of the capitalist mill. When some bloke with a big heart wanted to share the rewards of his labours with the public at large, he asked his broker to float the company on the Stock Exchange. That's what made the money go round and kept the sweaty palms of industry well greased. Nothing to do with passing the buck or paying the gas bill. But, of course, you can't believe everything you read in the papers.

Despite Brian's explanation, I was far from chuffed at losing half a million quid in the space of four or five months. Blimey! What would my old Mum have said? Sid, she would have said, you need your head examined. And maybe I do. Half a million quid is a lot of money to disappear into thin air. Of course, I'd had to benefit of a trip to Australia and I had put on a bit of weight, according to the scales in Mrs S.'s bathroom. But clearly I couldn't go on chucking money down the drain at this rate. Something had to be done. Leaving Brian, I returned to the City for a quiet chat with Siggy, my commodities broker.

Siggy was surprised to see me. He looked even more embarrassed than Freddy had when I turned up out of the blue to reclaim my bed in Fulham.

'This is a most unexpected pleasure,' he said, hurriedly closing the pages of a Smut-type magazine. 'Have a good trip?'

'Fine,' I said. 'How am I doing on the commodities front?'

Siggy poked at the screen in a half-hearted way. We flipped

through coffee, cocoa, sugar, metals and live hogs. I couldn't help noticing a shifty look creep into his eyes.

'We took a bit of a header on orange juice, I'm afraid,' he said. 'Since then, I've had to switch quite frequently to keep our head above water.'

'How much am I down?' I asked.

'Well, I can't tell you exactly without looking up the records,' said Siggy. 'But, at a guess, I'd say you probably had ten or twenty grand left.'

'Twenty grand left! But I gave you a hundred thousand, plus another ten grand to keep us afloat. Do you mean to say that all that has gone?'

Siggy drummed his fingers nervously on the desk.

'Well, as you know, Sid, commodities are a very high-risk business. You accepted as much when you signed the risk disclosure statement.'

'Yes, but I didn't know I was signing a blank cheque. I don't understand how you could have lost so much?'

'I can explain, if you like.'

'Please do.'

'Well, I admit we came unstuck over the orange juice contract. We were doing very nicely until along came this rumour that the Israelis had developed a new type of citrus, with twice the yield. You can imagine the effect of that on the market.'

'Why didn't you get out? You were supposed to be looking after my interests?'

'I did,' said Siggy. 'I switched immediately to cocoa, just as the Ghanaians announced that production was way ahead of forecast. So down went cocoa.'

Siggy surveyed three-month rubber and sighed.

'In fact, I wouldn't say there were many runners anywhere at the moment.'

'Just as well I'm not a betting man, then.'

Siggy lit a cigarette and inhaled deeply, removing a speck of tobacco from his tongue. The nicotine seemed to steady his nerves. I suppose that playing with other people's money is a great responsibility and must make you a bit edgy. After a few seconds he summoned up a smile.

'The charts are pointing to a sustained upswing in soyabeans pretty soon,' he said. 'I think there's a chance we could recover at least part of our losses if you'd put up, say, another fifty grand?'

I was tempted, I must admit. When you've lost as much as I had, you'd do anything to get some of it back. But something about Siggy's manner, his listlessness, his general lack of candour, made me hesitate.

'Can I see a record of my trades so far?' I asked. 'That'll help me weigh up the odds.'

'Bit awkward, just at the moment,' said Siggy, drawing nervously on the cigarette. 'We are having a spot of bother with the computer.'

'The screen seems to work all right,' I said.

'Different system,' said Siggy. 'Incompatible.'

'But you must have a record on the back of an envelope or somewhere?' I said.

I have always wondered what a computer could do that an envelope couldn't.

Siggy opened the bottom drawer of his desk and pulled out a wad of papers.

'We could go through these, I suppose, and try to work out something.'

'Fine,' I said. 'So long as we come up with a figure.'

I was amazed at how easily I was able to talk to these guys now. I suppose losing a few quid provides an incentive to converse.

Siggy spread out the papers on his desk. Each sheet contained details of the transactions undertaken on my behalf, buying this, selling that, switching out of a loss-making contract to one where the upside potential looked brighter. But, even when all the details had been transferred to the back of the envelope (and a sheet of paper, to be exact) the figures didn't add up.

'That leaves £38,000 unaccounted for,' I said. 'What have you done with that?'

'Well, of course,' said Siggy, stubbing out half a cigarette and reaching for another one, 'there are the costs of buying and selling. The £38,000 is my commission.'

'Your commission?'

I felt quite weak.

'I have lost sixty thousand quid and paid you thirty eight thousand pounds for the privilege of doing so?'

'I did point out that this was not a game for amateurs,' said Siggy, accidentally setting the wastepaper basket on fire as he dropped the lighted match. 'This is a high-risk business. If you'd made a hundred grand, you'd have thought £38,000 was peanuts.'

'But I haven't and it's not,' I countered. 'Now, if you think I am handing over thirty eight thousand quid for the pleasure of losing sixty grand, you have got another thought coming, mate.'

The aggressiveness that was never far below my surface now asserted itself. I was getting quite angry. I wondered what a Welsh rugby player would have done in the circumstances.

'Look,' said Siggy, 'let's not get hot under the collar about this. I admit I haven't done too well so, as a gesture of goodwill, I am prepared to refund you twenty grand, provided you leave it in the market.'

'So that you can lose it and charge more commission?' I cried. 'You must be joking.'

'With the £18,000 you have got left,' he said, indicating my net worth on the envelope, 'that would give you a stake of £38,000. In fact, to show my willingness to make amends, I'll say forty grand. Now, I can't be fairer than that, can I?'

'I'll tell you what you can do,' I said, standing up and preparing to leave. 'You can let me have a cheque for £38,000 and we'll call it a day. Commodity trading is for the birds.'

Siggy shrugged.

'All right,' he said. 'But I am sorry to hear it. I'll put a cheque in the post, just as soon as we have the computer on-stream and can work out the exact amount.'

I don't know why it needs a computer to work out something a Chinaman with a toy abacus could have done in thirty seconds but that's modern technology for you.

'I'm staying at the Inn on the Park,' I said. 'You can send it to me there.'

Siggy looked very sorry for himself. He was not, I realised, the world's most brilliant commodity trader. Now I understood why he was so anxious for me to sign the piece of paper when I first came to his office. A prime example of passing the parcel. The moral, I suppose, is to make sure you're not holding it when the music stops.

Well, Sid, I said to myself as I ambled somewhat aimlessly towards the Long Room, for a capitalist you're not doing too well in the enterprise society. On the other hand, the enterprise society is doing pretty well out of you. What you need is a sure-fire investment to restore your faith in the system. But what you need most of all is a double whisky to steady the nerves before you grab the first bowler-hatted git by the lapels and demand to know how much *he* paid in capital gains tax last year. The police might not take such a lenient view of assault and battery this time.

The Long Room was still pretty crowded, considering it was half past two and in a hard-working, enterprise society everybody with a job ought to have been hard at work. The head waiter pulled a bit of a face but nevertheless found room for me at a table covered with the debris of a previous meal. I noticed that whoever had dined there had left a fiver as a tip. A fiver! Somebody was doing all right, then. Probably a commodity broker, I thought vindictively.

After a steak and a glass of burgundy, I felt much better and less inclined to punch the nearest person on the nose. As I sat there with my coffee, I could hear these frightfully nice chaps at the table behind me discussing the financial affairs of others. One firm of brokers – no names, no pack drill, wink! wink! – was a bit behind with its payments. Could be a sign of something nasty. Best tread with caution. Well, how anybody in the City, especially commodity brokers, could be in trouble when they had the likes of me to support them I failed to see. And, if they were, tough luck. Those who fell by the wayside couldn't expect such much sympathy in a hard-nosed enterprise society.

I gave the waiter a quid and took a taxi back to the hotel. The time had arrived, I told myself, to give some serious thought to my investment strategy. But first I had to find somewhere decent to live.

13. Dear Abbey

Nothing, wrote Doctor S. Johnson (1709-1784), concentrates the mind so wonderfully as the prospect of imminent bankruptcy. I read that in one of those learned journals that cover the stock market. But he was right, you know. If you're going to go bust in a fortnight, and you're not broke at the moment, then you've got to do something about it. Some blokes reckon that, if it's in the stars, there's not much you can do. Inevitable, they say. Look at that Spitting Image chap in the United States. Put all his faith in the stars – and, by stars, I don't mean the bum actors he used to work with. He meant the Milky Way where the celestial forces meet to gang up on this little old planet of ours. And what about that Einstein fellow who reckoned you could even bend rays of light if there was enough dense matter in space?

Well, Sid, old son, I reckon there's a fair chunk of dense matter down here somewhere, not a million light years from yours truly, if you've managed to lose five hundred thousand quid in the space of a few months. But, quite honestly, I haven't got much faith in the stars. Do you remember that William Shakespeare, who, in his day, was what some people might call a teenage scribbler? He reckoned the stars had nothing to do with it. I quote: 'The fault, dear Brutus (Brutus was the bloke what helped to do in Julius Caesar), is not in our stars, but in ourselves, that we are underlings.' In other words, don't blame the broker when the market dips; blame yourself for not getting on the blower and screaming 'Sell!' Anyway, that's how I see it.

Of course, Shakespeare had nothing to do with Doctor Johnson. A bit before his time, as I recall. But, as they were both top-notch writers, I couldn't help thinking about them while I was having a drink at Ye Olde Cheshire Cheese, that pub off Fleet Street. I had gone there to see what makes these blokes on the Daily Smut behave in the way they do. But, of course, they've all packed up and gone now. To the wastelands of the East, somebody was saying. Removed themselves completely from the street of shame. So I never did find out. But as I was taking the air before catching the bus home I stumbled across this joint where the doc. was supposed to have lived. That's what got me thinking about it.

The main thing, I guess, is that it wasn't a bad looking pile of bricks and mortar. And, if it had lasted that long (the good doc. had been dead for two hundred years), it must have been a good investment. The more I thought of it, the more I remembered what my old grandmother used to say. 'Sid,' she'd say, even before she knew I had won the pools (which she never did, of course, being dead), 'you can't go wrong putting your money into bricks and mortar.' Mind you, her little pile of bricks and mortar were reduced to rubble by Herr Hitler but you can't blame her for that, I suppose. It was in her stars. But, with Hitler out of the way and Idi Amin some place where the gravitational pull of the moon wouldn't affect him, I figured it might not be such a bad idea to sink a few quid into a house, instead of just looking for somewhere to rent.

But where? That was the question. This bloke at the hotel, an American realtor, he said he was, reckoned I couldn't go wrong by investing in Florida. Great place, great climate, low maintenance, low taxes and, best of all, a weak dollar.

'What about the inhabitants?' I enquired. 'I wouldn't feel safe in my bed there.'

'No problem,' he said. 'All our properties are wired directly to the local police department. And, if you like, we can build you an electric fence, as well as provide round-the-clock personalised security, with armed guards and blood hounds. I don't think you'll have any trouble.'

'Quite honestly,' I said, 'I'd prefer to live in England and be burgled occasionally.'

'In that case, you'll want a property in London. Highest insurance rates in the country. Tell you what, I've got one or two nice little apartments down Wapping way. Fantastic value, for the Docklands. Why not have a look?'

I can't say I wasn't interested. After all, the old Docklands were only a stone's throw from the City and, in the event of a crisis, I could be there on the spot within a few minutes. From what the bloke said, the development embodied all that was best in the free enterprise system. No red tape, no traffic jams, no gazumping and no criminals (except one or two locals who refused to move out and make room for the new inhabitants).

'Terrific atmosphere,' said my friend, the realtor. 'Just like the old days when Britain was a great trading nation. A place where you can do your own thing and not give a damn about the neighbours. I'd live there myself except that I can't afford it.'

For the first time, I suspected there might be a catch to living in this capitalist paradise.

'Why not take a cab and have a look?' he suggested.

I did. Talk about upheaval! It reminded me of that place they built in the Brazilian jungle. Cut down all the trees to make way for skyscrapers. Trouble was that, when they had finished, only the rich could afford to live there. All the poor people had to make do with a shanty town on the outskirts. Only difference between Brazil and the Isle of Dogs was that here the poor lived in council houses. Even then, I noticed that one or two had a Porsche in the backyard.

And the prices! I had been told that inflation was under control. But all the estate agents I spoke to in Wapping and thereabouts told me that house prices were going up at the rate of 50 per cent a year. Maybe houses don't count where inflation is concerned. Even in places south of the river, like Dulwich, they had been roaring ahead. I suppose Mrs S. must have done quite well out of her little place in Fulham. Not being a property owner, it's not the sort of thing you keep track of every day.

Anyway, after a tramp up and down Wapping High Street and a trip on the light railway to view 'Europe's smartest complex of luxury flats' I decided that the Docklands were probably not for me. Sid, I said, as a working-class lad who has suddenly come into a bit of money, you'd stick out like a sore thumb down here. You might be one of the nouveau riche but, believe me, the neighbours would look down on you. They represent the cream of capitalist society. Besides, having seen how share prices can go down as well as up, I didn't like the feel of property in that neck of the woods. Too toppy, to use one of Bernie's pet phrases.

No, Sid, old son, what you need is a little place in the country. I mean, you don't have to travel up and down to the City every day so you don't need to be near the railway. That opened up a vast area, of course. I rather fancied Kent or Sussex, somewhere like that – not too rural, so that a bloke like me would be frightened to cross a field wearing a red shirt, but civilised enough to get the papers every day. Even in Sussex, you would need to check your portfolio.

Well, I don't know if you've ever been house-hunting but I can tell you it's not as easy as it looks. You can spend days and days looking at all the houses on an estate agent's book and still not find the place you want. Besides, some of these estate agents have got pretty vivid imaginations. I mean, if a property has got a sewage farm next to it, why not say so, instead of coming out with some codswallop like 'Ideal situation with the benefit of prevailing winds'? What happens if the wind does not prevail? It pongs, that's what it does, as I can tell you from personal experience. And then there was this place balanced on the edge of a ninety-foot cliff. 'Unhindered views of the sea', said the brochure. Blimey! If you opened the window the spray came right in and put salt on the taties whether you wanted it or not. One good earth tremor, I thought, and you'd be in the drink, furniture and all. Anyway, I wasn't all that fond of the sea, especially along coasts where swimmers were likely to come face to face with extraneous matter.

In the end, I settled for the country, just on the borders of Kent and Sussex. I was lucky in a way, I suppose. The bloke what was selling had been wiped out on the foreign exchange market. Put all his eggs in the German basket, then discovered that the Bank of England was still fighting the last war. So, down went his pfennig (he must have had a hell of a lot of them to be wiped out) and up went the shutters on his desirable country residence. I made an offer, two hundred grand, cash on the nail, no mucking about, and was not surprised when he accepted it. That's when the solicitors got in on the act and things started to go wrong.

I don't know what solicitors do but if you want to find problems where there aren't any problems – at least, none to speak of – hire yourself an attorney. He will find a problem for you and toss it around until he has shaken out all the loose change. Then, if you're lucky and he hasn't popped off to Cincinnati for the annual convention of the American Bar Association (as an observer, of course), you can get on with the job.

Lawyers are into all sorts of other rackets these days, like telling you what building society to patronise and even what insurance policy to take out. Seems to me that, like everybody else, they're too anxious to get their sticky little fingers in the enterprise pie. I mean, in the past, if you wanted legal advice (which most law-abiding citizens didn't) you went to a lawyer. If you wanted to buy insurance, you went to an insurance broker. If you wanted somebody to add up your losses, you went to a chartered accountant. Now, it seems, they can all do each other's jobs. Jacks of all trades. And you know what they say about that? Jacks of all trades and master of none.

Well, I won't bore you with all the legal niceties that my bloke managed to chuck in the air but it reminded me of one of those pictures you see, entitled 'Romanian peasants at harvest time'. One of them would throw the wheat into the air and the other would catch the chaff (or was it the other way about?). I wondered if my bloke had any Romanian blood, I can tell you. But, to be fair, he was able to advise me on the financial aspects of house purchase. Apparently, he was well in with one of those little building societies you can still find in country towns, if you look hard enough. Paid a little bit over the odds for deposits and therefore sucked in cash from old-age pensioners struggling to make ends meet.

'What you need is a non-status mortgage,' said Stubbs. 'Then they won't enquire into how much you earn. And, even if they do, just leave it to me. I'll send them an official letter.'

'But wouldn't it be best,' I said, 'seeing as how I've only three hundred grand left, to put at least two hundred into a house and get a roof over my head?'

'And what would you live on?' asked my solicitor. 'Grass?'

'I'd have thought one hundred thousand pounds was enough for a single bloke,' I said. 'I don't smoke, don't drink more than a bottle of champagne a day and haven't got a car. I don't give much to the Chancellor, I'm afraid.'

'Good man,' said Stubbs. 'But you miss the point. With house prices going up 30 per cent a year, it makes sense to borrow as much as you can at ten per cent. Then you make two hundred per cent on your money. Are you with me?'

'Not quite,' I said, bowing to the superior brain power of Romanian chaff catchers.

'Look,' he said, 'you put down a hundred grand, right? And you borrow a hundred grand at ten per cent. Your house goes up by 30 per cent – even more if you can spot where reason is in short supply. Profit on your investment, 30 per cent; profit on borrowed money, 200 per cent. And you've still got money in the bank to fiddle around with. Take a cruise, visit your uncle in Argentina . . . '

'I haven't got an uncle in Argentina,' I said.

'Never mind. Buy stocks and shares with it, then. As a matter of fact, the society has just done a deal with Eggemon and Co., the stockbrokers. They'll buy any shares you like – and at a very reasonable commission.'

'And how much do you get for introducing me to the society and, through them, to their broker?' I asked.

'Me? I don't get a penny, old boy,' said Stubbs, looking very hurt. 'I'm just acting in the best interests of my client, which happens to be you.'

'That's all right, then.'

I didn't like to tell him that the reason I was buying a house was to salvage a few pennies before the vultures could get their hands on them. But, after he had explained the arithmetic again, I could see there were advantages in borrowing money when you already had enough to buy a nice property. I wondered why more people didn't do it.

'They do, old boy, they do. Five billion quid promised last month, all to buy bricks and mortar – and maybe a carpet or two if the taxman's not looking. Take my advice: put down a deposit of a hundred grand, borrow the same amount and invest the balance in some high-yielding equities. You'll be set up for life.'

After my experiences in the high-risk sectors of the market so far, I had to admit it wasn't a bad idea. Perhaps lawyers could justify their incursion into the financial sector by providing the sort of prudent advice that was sadly missing elsewhere. I checked out of the Inn on the Park and moved into a smaller place in Tunbridge Wells (not quite as luxurious but one sixth of the price). While Stubbs was grappling with the complexities of the Land Registry, I shuffled along to the local branch of the Medway Building Society.

It wasn't one of the big ones, as the lawyer had warned. But it had a nice neon light that flashed an amber welcome and a window full of leaflets promising half a per cent more if you left your money there and not with one of the big boys across the street. And, as Stubbs had already revealed, they had a direct line to the stock market through Messrs. Eggemon and Co. No frills, just a plain, honest-to-goodness dealing service. Tell us what you want and we'll get it. Or, if you don't want it, we'll ditch it. At that moment, all I wanted was to open an account and lay the foundations for a mortgage.

The manager was extremely pleased to see me. I don't think he had seen a cheque for a hundred thousand quid before, especially one drawn on the Bank of Taiwan.

'One hundred thousand pounds will, of course, entitle you to our very top rate,' he explained, filling in the various forms to enroll me as a member. 'You won't do better anywhere, I can assure you.'

'So I understand.'

'Of course, our rates for borrowers are slightly higher, too. But you can't have it both ways, can you? Ha-ha!'

'How much higher?' I asked.

'About a quarter of one per cent,' he said. 'I think you will find that still leaves us very competitive.'

'Nothing in it, when you take into account property prices,' I agreed. 'But, surely, if you pay half a point more and charge only a quarter that must squeeze the margins?'

'We, sir, are a small building society and pride ourselves on our efficiency. We are not a public company with huge overheads and an advertising agent to support. Our aim is to provide loans for our members, not free shares for the masses.

At the Medway, we like to think we are still a cooperative.'

'Does that mean I can have a mortgage?'

'Subject to valuation and satisfactory references, of course. You wouldn't be investing here otherwise, would you?'

'Probably not,' I had to admit.

'How much did you have in mind?'

'About a hundred thou.'

The manager raised his eyebrows. I hoped he wasn't going to be one of those difficult types one meets in the provinces.

'You would like to borrow one hundred thousand pounds?'

'Yes. Haven't you got that much?'

'My dear sir!' he laughed. 'Of course we've got that much. And more. We're one of the fastest-growing societies in the country. It's just that one hundred thousand pounds is rather more than we normally advance.'

'You're in the big league now,' I said. 'You're lucky, I was going to pay cash until my solicitor advised me not to.'

The manager stared at me, as though trying to assess my status in the financial community.

'If you've got any spare cash,' he said at last, 'might I recommend a small investment via our dealing service? Government stocks are offering a fairly high return at the moment.'

Government stocks. Now, why hadn't I thought of those in the first place? I'd been into foreign bonds, foreign exchange (that reminded me, I must see how Barry was doing), aboriginal land rights, commodity futures and Saudi pudding companies. But never, but never, into the stocks issued by the very government which had been so kind to we millionaires. It was only right that I put a few quid their way.

The trouble with gilts, though, is that the potential for capital growth is limited. And capital growth was what I wanted. Even a pools winner cannot rely on a steady income from interest rates well into double figures. Suppose the socialists got in? They would slash the rates before you could say Denis Healey. And down would come the pound, competitiveness and all. No, despite my desire to reward a government that encouraged entrepreneurs, I had to spread the risk.

'Tell you what,' I said to the manager, who was waiting expectantly. 'I've got a spare bob or two. Why not buy me fifty thousand quid's worth of investment trusts? I hear they do pretty well.'

'Any trust, sir, or will you leave that to the broker?'

'I'll rely on his discretion,' I said. 'But I want one that goes for growth.'

'Very good, sir. And just as soon as your property transaction is complete you can bank on us for the mortgage.'

That, I thought, was a strange expression for a building society to use – you can bank on us – although I do know that some of them regard themselves as banks these days. What with cheque books, cash dispensers, personal loans and all the rest of it, I suppose it won't be long before they start charging for their services, especially if they have a few shareholders to support.

Funny creatures, building societies. My old man said that years ago, if you wanted to buy a house, you had to go down on bended knee and almost beg for the money. And even if they decided you could have some you had to join a queue and save with them for yonks before they actually handed it over. Now, you just walk into any branch and the manager brings out the red carpet and pleads with you to take his money. They've got so much they don't know what to do with it. Cars, yachts, holidays, home improvements; just ask and the money's yours. Well, not exactly yours because they always want it back. But nobody's going to worry so long as house prices keep going up.

A mate of mine had one of these junk mail circulars come through the door. Please borrow our money, it said. You can do anything you like with it so long as you don't pay us back for at least ten years. From a building society it was, too, not one of these shysters you see offering personal loans in the paper. And do you know what? They only charged 34 per cent for money left on deposit by the likes of me who earned eight or nine per cent (or nine and a half in the case of the Medway). Blimey! No wonder they can afford junk mail. If they ever went public, you'd be on to a winner.

Mind you, anybody who borrows at that rate must be pretty

desperate. And if you're desperate you're probably none to fussy about repayments. They must have a fair number of bad debts, I reckon. But we're in the realm of political economy here and I must confess I don't really understand it. Doesn't seem right to me, though, that building societies – which were set up to help the poor build houses for themselves – should be trying to put decent, law-abiding loan sharks out of business. Another example of the jack-of-all-trades society we now live in, I suppose. I wonder how they describe 34 per cent in the balance sheet? Usury, I'd call it, although I daresay a PR man like Frank could find a better word to stop the customers getting worried.

I'm rambling on a bit because you'll know, if you've ever bought a house, that it does take time for solicitors to earn their fee and down here in the country there's not much to do. That was one thing about Fulham: you could always nip up to the graveyard to have a look at Mother or the drilling rig or just generally watch life go by. In fact, it was about time I paid a social call on Mrs S., I thought, just to show that I hadn't forgotten the mattress and to collect any mail that may have arrived. So I took the train to Victoria and splashed out on a taxi to Fulham.

Freddy opened the door.

'Hullo, old boy!' he beamed. 'How nice to see you! Do come in. Isobel and I were just about to have a cup of tea. You will join us, won't you?'

Freddy seemed jolly pleased with himself, I thought. I wondered if he had found a new client or whether the exchange had dropped its investigation. Mrs S. was in the kitchen, preparing a small snack.

'Sid!' she cried, clasping me to her bosom like a long-lost friend. 'How nice to see you!'

As it was only a couple of weeks since I had last seen her, I thought her welcome was a little bit on the enthusiastic side. But, I must say, it was quite a nice sensation being squeezed by Mrs S. Fortunately, she was not wearing the opal brooch I had given her.

'How's things at the exchange?' I asked casually as we

devoured our smoked salmon and brown bread canopies.

'Oh, say no more about it, old boy,' replied Freddy breezily. 'A complete misunderstanding. They really ought to get some people in the surveillance department who know the difference between a coincidence and a raw deal. All over, I'm glad to say. I assume,' he added, 'they didn't get in touch with you?'

'Not a word,' I said.

'Good!' cried Freddy. 'Excellent!'

'Almost as good as our other news,' said Mrs S.

'Other news?'

'Shall I tell him or will you, my love? After all, you're his broker.'

'My Bongo bonds have come good?' I said hopefully.

"Fraid not,' said Freddy. 'No, the fact is that Isobel and I have decided to get married. We have arranged a little ceremony at the registry office the week after next. You will be able to come along, I hope?'

Well, I was flabbergasted! Absolutely dumbfounded. I couldn't speak.

'Oh, dear! I hope the news hasn't upset you?' laughed Mrs S. 'I was hoping you'd be a witness.'

'No, no,' I stammered. 'Just surprised, that's all. A bit of a shock, really.'

'Bit of a shock to me as well, old boy, I don't mind telling you. Who'd have thought that old Freddy would have succumbed to the charms of a lady at his time of life?'

'Go on with you!' said Mrs S., poking him in the ribs. 'Didn't you say that I was a fine-looking woman?'

'I did, indeed,' Freddy confirmed. 'A fine-looking woman.'

'And a fine figure of a man, too, if I may say so,' I remarked. 'You'll be a fine-looking couple and maybe have a whole tribe of fine-looking kids.'

'Not at my time of life, old boy,' said Freddy. 'The last thing I want is a pile of nappies billowing in the Fulham breeze.'

I thought Mrs S. looked a bit disappointed but she said nothing.

'I'll be delighted to come along and be your best man or whatever you like,' I said. 'Where are you going to live, by the way?'

'We did think,' said Mrs S., 'that now they haven't struck oil in the cemetery we might buy one of the houses there – when they put them up, of course.'

'Isobel rather likes the idea of living where her mother had lain at rest for so long,' explained Freddy.

'It's comforting, really,' added Mrs S., 'even though she is not there any more. By the way, the rabbi was very impressed by the tombstone. It looks really nice, doesn't it, my dear?'

'Spot on,' said Freddy.

I wondered how they were going to pay for the house, which, even in a recycled graveyard, would cost a small fortune in London. But, still, that was their business and I didn't like to interfere. I expect they would sell the house in Fulham and get a fairly large mortgage. Should I tell them about my society or would that be too expensive for them? I expect Freddy had contacts. So I kept quiet.

On the way home, still feeling slightly dazed by news of the impending nuptials, I bought an Evening Standard from the vendor outside Charing Cross station. Some political scandal had made the front page again. We were just pulling out of Waterloo when I saw the headline on the financial page. SIB probes commodity broker. The SIB, in case you didn't know, stands for Securities and Investments Board and, if the truth be known, were probably responsible for making poor old Freddy sweat buckets of blood over the past week or two. I quickly cast an eye over the small print.

'Dectectives from the City fraud squad today raided the offices of Windrush Commodities,' the story read, 'following a tip-off about irregular dealings.

'They had been hoping to interview Mr Sigmund Bergstresser, the client services manager. But Mr Bergstresser, 34, of Geneva, did not turn up for work today.

'Police and immigration officials have been alerted although it is thought that Mr Bergstresser, who is known to have a villa on the Costa del Sol, may already have left the country.

'According to well-informed sources, Windrush has been late in settling client accounts. About £3 million is thought to be involved.'

As I said, I was already a bit groggy, trying to absorb the shock of Mrs S.'s wedding, and at first I didn't recognise Siggy's name. If they'd have said Siggy, I'd have cottoned on straight away. By now, I was feeling more than groggy; I was feeling pretty goddamned sick. If only I'd have known before Waterloo, I could have jumped out and whooshed down the Drain to the City. But, here I was, speeding through the Kent countryside, while the cops were no doubt prying into my personal affairs, with a watching brief from the Inland Revenue. I wondered whether to get off at Sevenoaks and go back. But what could a bloke do in a situation like that? I decided to continue my journey and have a stiff drink when I got home.

The cops were waiting when I arrived at the hotel. Contrary to regulations, they were having a wee drinkie themselves, on the house, as it turned out.

'Mr Arbuthnot?' said this tall, thin guy in a pin-striped suit as I asked for my key.

'Yes?'

'Could we have a word with you, sir? In private.'

'You had better come up.'

That's when I knew the proprietor began to have doubts about me. Of course, the cops didn't say what they were there for; just wanted a word with Mr Arbuthnot. That's how rumours start and folks get the wrong end of the stick.

I asked Room Service to bring us a pot of tea and a double whisky.

'We are sorry to bother you, sir,' the officer who had already damaged my credit rating said, 'but we believe that you are – or were – a client of Windrush Commodities?'

'Yes. I read about it in the train.'

'Then you'll know that Mr Bergstresser has done a bunk?'

'So they say.'

'With all the firm's money, as far as we can make out.'

I did not reply. How could Siggy, who was making enough money out of me, anyway, do this to me? I felt as sick as a parrot.

'All we were wondering, sir, is whether you could identify these papers?' – he opened his Filofax and drew out a wad of bumff – 'and confirm them as being an accurate record of your trading with the company?'

He passed the papers as the maid came in with the pot of tea, and what they called a Garden of England assortment. Cream cakes, that sort of thing. I downed the whisky in one gulp.

I glanced through the computer print-out. At least, they had managed to get the electronic brain working again. There were several pages and none of them seemed to be in focus.

'You seem to have been a very active trader, sir. And, if I may say so, not a particularly successful one.'

I didn't like the way he said that. What would a bloody cop know about the machinations of the commodity markets, even if he was in the fraud squad? I tried to think of a suitable reply but the old brain was a bit fuddled.

'I don't know what you mean, officer,' I said.

(Why do people call the fuzz officers when most of them are not of commissioned rank? Maybe it has something to do with the fact that most of them sit in the office, doing the work of clerical officers, when they should be out on the beat.)

'What I mean is, sir, that according to these records, you are a quarter of a million in the red.'

'Don't be bloody daft,' I said. 'Where d'you get that from?'

'From here, sir,' he said, pointing to the current balance on the final page of the print-out which I hadn't reached yet. 'Closing daily balance, 249,616 pounds debit.'

'That's ridiculous,' I said. 'They couldn't have fixed the computer. If I'd been that much down, they – that is, Siggy – would have been in touch.'

'Is he a friend of yours, sir?'

'Not if he has run off with my money, he isn't.'

'As I was trying to explain, sir, he hasn't run off with your money; only the firm's money. But, as you seem to be the largest debtor, we were wondering whether you had any plans to join him?'

'Now, listen, officer,' I said. 'I've had a very stressful day. I've not only discovered that my ex-landlady is marrying my stockbroker but I read in the paper that my ex-commodity broker has gone missing. Now you come here, drink my tea, eat my cakes and suggest that I am about to board a plane for Malaga.'

'I didn't say anything about Malaga, sir. Is that where you were intending to go?'

'I am intending to go nowhere,' I said. 'What's more, I doubt if I could afford to go anywhere now.'

'You were simply a client of the firm, is that it, sir?' the other fellah said, speaking for the first time.

'Simply a client,' I said. 'A client hoping to make his fortune out of cotton futures.'

'Is that why you were buying jute?' asked the smart-arse with the Filofax. 'As far as I can see, you have been buying everything but cotton, sir.'

At that stage, I must have been pretty ill because all I can remember is staring at the print-out and wondering how the hell I could have been two hundred and forty nine thousand quid in the red. What had Siggy been doing with my money?

'If I were you, sir, I'd get on to your accountant straight away, because if the firm goes bust, which it seems very likely to do, and you're shown on the books as a debtor, you might have to cough up more than you had intended. You know what creditors are like when they demand a pound of flesh.'

Well, I could see the guy was trying to be helpful. Obviously, he had summed me up as yet another poor slob who had been taken for a ride by a cowboy in the commodities market. I offered him a cucumber sandwich from the Garden of England.

'No, thank you, sir,' he said. 'We must be getting back. But we may wish to contact you again. You'll be staying here for some time?'

'Until my house is ready.'

'You are buying a property in the area, sir?'

'Trying to.'

'Would you mind giving me the address?'

I gave him the address.

'Thank you, sir. We'll get back to the City now. And thank you for the tea.'

'You're welcome,' I said.

The trouble with living in a small country hotel, as opposed to slumming it in a large one, is that everybody knows your business. The cops had been the soul of discretion but I could see when I came down to dinner that everybody, just everybody, knew that I was the subject of a police investigation. The landlord was right snooty.

'I was wondering, sir,' he said, as I was going up to my room after a most unsatisfactory meal, 'whether you might like to settle your account to date? We try not to let bills mount up, you understand?'

I understood all right. I gave him a cheque on the Bank of La Paz. That made him think.

Well, to cut a long story short, the police picked up Siggy before he could even get out of London. He had been holed up in one of those expensive matchboxes on the Thames, just upstream from the cement factory. He had driven to Dagenham to pick up some fish and chips and was on the way home when his Porsche broke down. The local bobby recognised him as he peered under the bonnet looking for the engine. Poor Siggy never did know whether he was coming or going.

And, of course, once they'd got the thumbscrews on him at Wood Street he broke down and spilled the beans. Not ordinary beans; soybeans. Siggy, it seemed, had been trying to make a killing – the gambler's desperate last throw. But, in the commodities game, you've got to be smarter than the next guy all the time. One false step and you end up like me, with a debit balance. Brian, my accountant, explained it all to me after he had moved pretty swiftly to make sure I was not lumbered with a chunk of Windrush debts. We got Stubbs to put in an affidavit saying that Siggy had bought and sold in my name and without authority and, furthermore, after I had told him to close my account. I mean, can you imagine anybody throwing good money after bad in the commodity markets?

14. Call the fire brigade

Lightning, they say, never strikes in the same place twice. That's why, if you find an old oak tree with a deep scar from a previous encounter, you can feel pretty relaxed about standing under it while the storm rages around you. According to theory, your tree is the safest spot in the forest. What they don't tell you is that, thanks to the afore-mentioned dose of high-speed electricity, the waterlogged bough over your head is liable to come crashing down. And when you try to explain to the hard-pressed sister on the casualty ward just why you've got splinters up your bum and oak leaves sprouting from the earholes, you get pretty short shrift. It's much the same in the financial services sector. It is quite possible for lightning to strike not only twice but to run along the ground at a great rate of knots to the very spot where you are sheltering from the rain.

As I was contemplating the dreadful wrath of nature and the remarkable lack of sympathy for those who lose their money in the stock market, I had a call from Stubbs, my lawyer.

'I've got everything lined up,' he said. 'We should be able to exchange contracts in a day or two, if that's all right with you?'

'Fine by me,' I said. 'The sooner I can move out of the hotel, the better.'

'You'll need a small deposit,' he warned. 'Twenty thousand quid, to be exact.'

'No problem,' I replied. 'It's all in the building society.'

'Splendid!' cried Stubbs. 'Then I'll be in touch.'

The prospect of getting a roof over my head was almost as exciting as becoming a shareholder for the first time. A house, they say, is likely to be the greatest single drain on your resources you'll ever know. That wasn't quite true in my case, of course, but I guess most people have not got a string of brokers to support. At least it gave me a toehold in the great property-owning democracy that had arisen from an enterprise culture. I called on Brian, my accountant in Penge, to check the state of Sid Enterprises.

'You're getting a bit low on the readies,' he said. 'By the time you've paid the full deposit, a hundred thou., and invested another fifty, you won't have much left. And most of that's in the foreign exchange market.'

I had completely forgotten about Barry, who had been juggling currencies on my behalf for the past couple of months. I decided to make a flying visit to the forex desk that afternoon, as soon as I could escape from Penge.

'I've had a run of bad luck,' I said to Brian, hoping to explain my straitened circumstances.

'A bad run of something,' said Brian.

'I suppose one can't go through life winning all the time,' I observed philosophically. 'I won nearly a million quid on the swings. Now it's roundabout time.'

'At least you've got the security of bricks and mortar, I wouldn't mind living in that part of the country myself.'

'You must come down for the weekend once I've settled in. We'll crack a bottle of champagne.'

'Super!' exclaimed Brian. 'I'll look forward to it.'

After an inferior sandwich at the local hostelry, I took the train to the City. Barry actually worked for one of these American banks that are a force to be reckoned with in the foreign exchange market. I remember reading how some of them had got their fingers caught in the grille when some kraut bank (not mine) collapsed in a heap several years ago. Must have taught them a useful lesson, I suppose. Next time, they'll heed the warning signals before their balance sheet looks like the moths have been at it.

While I was waiting in the foyer, I glanced at the ticker tape that the bank had provided for its customers. Quite a marvel of technology, really. There was this little machine, buzzing like an angry bee as it churned out a stream of company news and stock market reports. I noticed the latest cricket score from Karachi or some such place. England wasn't doing terribly well again. ICI profits were up, soybeans were down. There was a long piece headed 'Regulatory authority determined to stamp out malpractice' and another entitled 'Bank warns of credit flood'. There was even a paragraph about the arrest of Siggy.

Again remanded in custody on a charge of embezzling £3 million.

Then another item caught my eye. 'Police investigate building society'. I read on. 'Kent police are investigating the sudden closure of all three branches of the Medway Building Society in the county. In Canterbury, investors trying to withdraw funds smashed a window and damaged a neon light. A spokesperson for the society, which has been growing rapidly in recent months, declined to comment.'

'Mr Arbuthnot?'

I turned. A messenger poised to clamp a name tag on my lapel was waiting to escort me to the dealing room. At least, I assumed he was. I don't remember any more because I must have fainted. When I came to, a bank official was plying me with brandy. And for a bank official to do that the situation must have been serious.

'Shall I call a doctor?' he asked anxiously.

'No, just my accountant.'

'I beg your pardon?'

'I'll be all right,' I said, touched by his concern.

I had another nip of the brandy. Five star stuff, too.

'I'm sorry,' I said. 'I've just had some bad news.'

'Do you have an account at the bank?' asked Florence Nightingale.

'No, just a foreign exchange position.'

'I'm sure the dealer will be only too happy to explain.'

'Later,' I said. 'First, I must call my solicitor.'

'In that case, everything I have said must be regarded as strictly without prejudice.'

I don't know what he was talking about and I hadn't time to argue. I could hear the call of the wild woods.

'Do you think you could grab me a taxi?' I asked.

'Certainly, sir.'

I don't remember much about the journey home except that the Weald of Kent looks pretty grotty when you've just blown a fortune. As soon as I arrived at the hotel I called Stubbs. He was round in a flash. One ear was plugged into a transistor radio. He looked very pale.

'This could be serious,' he said. 'Very serious.'

Well, I didn't need a lawyer to tell me that. Even in my shell-shocked state, I could see that the situation was beyond a joke.

'Very serious,' he muttered again. 'There's a lot of money at stake here.'

'Mr Stubbs,' I said firmly, 'I am perfectly well aware that a lot of money is at stake. That's why I called you round. What are you going to do about it?'

'Well, there's not much we can do, I'm afraid,' the law officer confessed. 'We can only hope that the horse hasn't bolted and left the stable door wide open.'

He held up his hand to indicate that something was coming over the air waves.

'The trustees have called in receivers,' he said. 'That's serious, very serious.'

He turned a doleful eye in my direction.

'That could be very awkward,' he admitted. 'You were due to exchange contracts tomorrow.'

'Just a minor obstacle,' I said.

He brightened.

'You have money elsewhere?'

'Oh, yes,' I replied airily. 'I've got stacks of it tucked away here and there – in foreign currencies, in Bongo bonds, in holes in the ground . . . '

I almost said 'under the mattress' but he might have asked whose mattress and got the wrong idea.

'Then you'll be able to pay my fee?' he asked quickly.

'Possibly,' I said.

'That's all right, then. We don't want to start applying for legal aid at this stage of the game. But it's still very serious, I'm afraid.'

He paused and removed the plug from his ear.

'I knew this sort of thing was bound to happen sooner or later,' he said. 'Once you start upping the rates and competing with each other to lend money on secondhand cars instead of bricks and mortar you're asking for trouble. I mean, how could you possibly run a society on a margin of one quarter of one per cent when even the bloody typist demands ten thousand a year?

193

I know we can't compete in the legal profession with salaries like that.'

My sympathies at that precise moment in time were not with the legal profession, I must admit. They were with Sid, Sid Arbuthnot, whose faith in the property-owning democracy had been rocked to its very foundations. How could a first-time buyer, without even the tenure of a council house to fall back on, be robbed of his last quarter of a million? What were the so-called watchdogs doing about it? Yapping at strangers, I suppose. Why was it poor old Sid who kept getting bitten? Why had he not put all his money into ICI, as he had felt like doing, and have been done with it? He would at least have had a dividend cheque by now.

'There'll be an enquiry into this,' Stubbs muttered darkly. 'Somebody will go to jail.'

That'll provide work for a lawyer somewhere, I thought. Probably several lawyers, not to mention a judge or two, and maybe even a financial adviser who would be called in as an expert witness to explain to the jury how a building society in the prosperous south-east of England could go bust. With Sid's money in the vault. But I said nothing. There seemed nothing to say.

'At least the fifty thou. you put into investment trusts via Messrs. Eggemon and Co., ought to be safe,' said Stubbs, 'assuming that the order was placed in time.'

'And if it wasn't?'

Stubbs shrugged resignedly. His shoulders were beginning to reveal signs of a legal stoop.

'If it wasn't . . . then I'm afraid the money will still be on the books of the society.'

'Which means?'

'Which means that you'll have a hell of a job to get it back from the receivers. Of course, if you had invested directly through a stockbroker and not via an intermediary you would have been all right.'

'As I recall, it was you who recommended me to invest my money with the Medway?' I said.

'Not recommended,' said Stubbs, shuffling his feet as

though engaged upon some sort of ritual dance. 'Suggested. There is a world of difference between recommending somebody to put money into a society or fund and merely suggesting that he does so. You do understand the distinction, don't you?'

'Not really,' I confessed. 'Sounds very much the same thing to me. If I had gone to an intermediary and he suggested that I put my money into an offshore fund in, say, Gibraltar, I would think that he had recommended me to do it.'

Stubbs was looking very uncomfortable. I wondered if he had placed any money with the Medway.

'There is, I can assure you, a legal distinction,' he said. 'I would not want you to get up in court and say that Mr Stubbs *recommended* you to invest in the Medway. That would not be the case at all. But if you said that, upon enquiring where a safe place might be for the temporary deposit of funds, that Mr Stubbs suggested that you could lodge a little money there, in anticipation of getting a mortgage, that would be an accurate reflection of the facts, would it not?'

'If you say so.'

'I do say so. Now, do you think it would be worth our while to whizz down to the local office, just to see if there's any chance of having a quiet chat with somebody?'

'What do you think? Would you recommend it?'

Stubbs shot me a quick and, I thought, unfriendly glance.

'No, I can't honestly say that I would recommend it,' he said. 'I think we will just have to await the news. If it's any consolation to you,' he added, 'I have a few quid there myself.'

The news was not long in forthcoming. The papers next day were full of it. Medway insolvent, reported the Daily Telegraph. Hundreds lose life savings in building society crash, spelled out the Guardian. Home loans scandal, splashed the Mail. Kinky Kenneth in housing rip-off, observed the Smut. Even the F.T. had a story on the front page and a learned article, complete with graphs, on the inside. 'When will investors learn,' asked the F.T., 'that a fast-growing company – or, indeed building society – offering over the odds for cash is displaying the classic danger signs?' Well, I thought, it's all very well for the clever bastards in Fleet Street to pontificate after the event. But, if they're so clever, why didn't they draw our attention to the classic danger signals before now?

So that's it, then, I thought. At least I wouldn't have to explain why I couldn't exchange contracts for the purchase of a desirable residence in the country. There it was, all over the papers. Circumstances beyond my control. Stubbs could write a letter to the other fellow's lawyers, apologising for any inconvenience that may have been caused. I felt really sorry for the poor guy who had already lost a packet in the foreign exchange market. But, in an enterprise society, you have to look after Number One. I had my own foreign exchange position to worry about. There was no alternative but to pull out and rescue what remained of my funds. But first I called on Brian for a quick update on my net worth.

'Well, Sid, old son,' he said, in jocular fashion, 'the cupboard's beginning to look a bit bare.'

Just how bare he proceeded to demonstrate on his electronic calculator.

'I think it would be prudent to write off the entire amount placed with the Medway,' he said. 'You might get something back if one of the bigger societies can be persuaded to pick up the tab. But I doubt it.'

'Why would they want to do that?' I asked.

'Image,' explained Brian. 'Not good for the movement. Damages public confidence to have a society go down the pan, even if it is a grubby little outfit that ought to have been closed down by the DTI years ago.'

I wondered how Frank was getting on with his image-building exercise down under.

'And then there's the Australian debacle,' said Brian, as though reading my thoughts. He keyed in some more figures.

'And don't forget the Bongo affair,' I said, recalling my contribution to Britain's foreign aid budget.

'I won't,' said Brian. 'Unfortunate case of mistaken identity there. But, you never know, if you live long enough, you might get something back.'

'I'll keep taking the tablets,' I said.

We went through the entire portfolio, subtracting losses from trial balances and juggling with double-entry commission. But, no matter how hard we tried, assets continued to shrink.

'At least you won't have to pay capital gains tax,' Brian confirmed. 'But we ought to take steps to establish your losses so that they can be carried forward.'

Like the poor, capital losses are apparently always with you.

'Of course,' said Brian, 'life would be a lot simpler if you didn't have all these bank accounts all over the place. Now that you don't need to spread the risk so much, why not consolidate them all into one account?'

Well, that was the first decent idea I'd heard for some time. I wasn't exactly making a fortune in the high-interest ledger stakes these days. But which bank? That was the question. The Jews of Malta or the merchants of Venice? I'd had my fill of the listening bank, the action bank, the no-charges-if-you're-good bank, the woe-betide-you-if-you're-not bank and all the other licensed U.K. deposit-taking institutions. It's a pity that Villi, the two-metre kraut, had disappeared without trace. I had rather taken a shine to him. I was sorely tempted to open a brand new account with the American bank that kept a bottle of brandy for the use of clients in distress. The manager there must have had a heart somewhere. But they already had my foreign exchange business and I still had some risk to spread. In the end, I decided to remain with the jet set.

'I'll have everything transferred to the Bank of La Paz,' I said.

'Fine,' said Brian. 'That only leaves a hundred grand in foreign currency to worry about. You could still pull that out and use it to buy a house.'

'And what would I live on?' I asked. 'Grass?'

I must say, none of the foreign banks seemed to lose much sleep over the fact that I was closing my account with them. You'd have thought that, if they really valued their customers and wanted to remain on good terms with them, they might have shed a tear or two. But not even a wimper. Certainly, sir, with pleasure, sir. We'll pop your closing statement in the post. And, don't forget, if you're not satisfied with your new arrangements, you can always come back to us. Too much money around, I suppose. Easy come, easy go.

You can imagine that I was very relieved to find that Barry, the foreign exchange dealer, was still beavering away and that neither he had done a bunk nor had the bank collapsed around him. Mind you, he seemed very busy. The spot peso was dancing around in a way that suggested imminent devaluation and he had got a position open that he was anxious to close. At last, I managed to grab his attention.

'How's it going?' I asked.

'How's what going?'

'My investment.'

'Oh, well, I can't tell you exactly. But I think we're ahead.'

'That's the best news I've heard since Bongo turned out to be in South America,' I said.

'You're in dollars at the moment,' said Barry, pulling the plug on the peso. 'The one-month dollar-yen rate in Tokyo looked like a good bet so I put the lot in there.'

'And it's still there?'

'Not physically, of course,' said Barry, mildly surprised. 'It's all done by computer now.'

He nodded towards a screen that made as much sense to me as a bingo card after a bender.

'I'll check on it, if you like, and let you have a statement.'

'If you would,' I said. 'My accountant is getting anxious.'

'Old Brian? Getting anxious? I don't believe it.'

'Well, even if he's not, I am.'

'Very good, sir. I'll drop you a line tomorrow. In fact, I think we're about due to close the position, anyway.'

I don't know if you're familiar with the balance of payments situation in the United States. If not, let me explain. While we in Britain are fortunate to have a Chancellor who can balance the books with his eyes shut, they are not so fortunate in the United States. Over there, they are so rich they can afford to run this thing called a budget deficit. In other words, the books don't balance, even with the help of the Treasury computer. And, to judge by the size of the deficit, they never will balance until they put up taxes, which they won't, because nobody wants to make the pips squeak. But they also have this thing called a trade deficit. It seems that the little yellow bastards who make all the televisions and video cameras are quite happy to trade with the United States so long as the Americans don't try to sell anything to them. This naturally puts a strain on the U.S. balance of payments.

To be honest, I didn't realise there were two deficits in the United States until I heard this bloke on the BBC explain it. I don't think he realised, either, because he seemed to be back-pedalling an awful lot in an effort to make sense. The upshot, though, was that both these deficits were getting a bit out of hand. Of course, it didn't help when the Department of Trade in Washington was forced to admit that, owing to a computer error, the United States had imported ten times more Japanese motorcycles the previous month than had been shown in the official figures. Somebody had apparently had their eyes shut when the computer put the decimal point in the wrong place. Now, you don't have to be an economic whizz kid, or even employed by The Spectator, to see that the decimal point was going to affect my dollar position in Tokyo.

And it was just my luck that when I got back to the hotel the radio announced that the word 'deficit' had been struck out of the vocabulary as far as Britain was concerned. In future, said some bright spark at the Treasury, the country would live within its means. Exporting could be such fun and frightfully good for the pound sterling. I didn't know how good because when I phoned Barry to check he had gone home.

I can tell you this much, though. When he came back in the morning the dollar had slipped three and a half cents against the pound – which wouldn't have been so bad, he explained, if he hadn't taken a punt on the spread. It was a bit like investing in commodity futures, he said. You didn't have to put up the full amount; you just had to make sure you could afford the movements. That meant you could buy a whole bagful of dollars so long as you could cover the loss when the time came to sell. In my case, I discovered, I was the owner of five million dollars in Tokyo which had suddenly lost three per cent of their value.

'What's the cable! What's the cable!' Barry kept shouting.

The cable, I learned, was how they describe the dollar when it comes over the wire. I couldn't see much difference between a dollar on the wire and a dollar on the screen. Both seemed to be sinking under the weight of Japanese motorcycles and British initiative.

Of course, had we bought three months forward instead of a mere one month, we might have had room to breathe. But the position, as Barry kept reminding me, had to be closed by the end of the day. In the circumstances, I was compelled to remind him that it might have been wiser to have got out with time to spare and perhaps even a profit.

'How did I know they would make a cock-up with the computer?' he asked. 'It's like trying to predict when we'll join the snake.'

One thing you soon learn about the foreign exchange market is that they fly by the seat of their pants. No deep research; all gut reaction. In the old days, before the pound was allowed to bob around like a yo-yo on a yuppie's yacht, the Bank of England kept a pretty sharp eye on it. You could gamble – that is to say, take a view – on its performance within a clearly-defined margin. If it looked like hitting the buffers, the bank would take control. Now, of course, even the mark can be ripped to pieces by a pack of hungry wolves looking for something to chew.

I was still trying to figure out what five million times three cents was when there was a groan from the dealing desk.

'No sign of Bundesbank support!' cried a bird – not my type – near the teleprinter. 'Spot yen 136 Singapore.'

I saw Barry take out a handkerchief and wipe his brow. It was all double Dutch to me but the dealers seemed to know what the bird was on about. As far as I could make out, the dollar was going down all over the place. And so were my profits.

Well, I couldn't stay there all day. The tension was too great. I could see why foreign exchange dealers were worn out at twenty six. Barry, I thought, must have been about thirty. I left and installed myself at the bar in Balls Bros. One could always find out what was happening in the markets from there. To my surprise, Freddy had emerged from hiding and was enjoying a bottle of claret.

'Hullo, old boy!' he cried, shaking my hand. 'Let me get you a glass. Bad show about young Siggy, what? Would never have expected it of him. Must have been under frightful pressure.'

'Either that or he was just bent,' I said.

'Siggy, bent? Well, I don't know. Who's to say that we all aren't bent in some way? Look at that fellah Oscar Wilde. Forced to write poetry with a prison pencil just because he had a weak link somewhere. Still, I don't think Siggy was that way inclined. I suppose you'll have to give evidence?'

'Probably,' I said.

'Bad luck, really, having to bare your financial soul in open court. Ought to be a law against it.'

'How's the wedding coming along?' I asked, hoping to change the subject.

'Oh, fine, just fine,' said Freddy. 'Isobel is getting all excited, of course. But you can't rush these things. How's your own house-hunting coming along?'

I told him about the Medway Building Society.

'Oh, bad show. I'm awfully sorry. Here, let me top you up.'

'Thanks.'

It was the first time I had ever seen Freddy with a bottle of his own. I hoped the prospect of marriage hadn't driven him to drink.

'Tell you what,' he said. 'There's a little placing coming up shortly by a house I'm on friendly terms with. I'll see if I can get you a few.'

'What's a placing?' I asked.

'New issue,' said Freddy. 'But instead of offering it to the public they keep it within the family. Normally, of course, you wouldn't get any. But they owe me a favour. I'll see what I can do.'

'Thanks,' I said. 'But I'm not sure I can afford to lose any more money. I'm practically down to loose change now.'

'You won't lose, old boy. That's the whole point. It's virtually a guaranteed way of making money. That's why, in the normal course of events, they'd give it to their friends. But leave it to me. I'll put in a word on your behalf.'

He drained his glass and pushed the bottle towards me.

'Must rush, old boy. Got a client waiting for some advice.'

I looked at my watch. Nearly three. Only two hours to sell my dollars unless I wanted to take delivery and pay for them. But where, I asked, would I get five million bucks on a Friday afternoon? Unless miracles happened I was going to have to cough up the difference. The bloke at the next table had a calculator.

'Excuse me,' I said. 'But could you tell me what five million times three cents is?'

'Three per cent of five mil. is a hundred and fifty thou.,' he said, without so much as pressing the all clear on his little machine. 'Taken a punt on the dollar, eh?'

'Just a small one,' I confessed.

'Pretty dangerous these days,' he said, 'with all these cowboys in the market. I wouldn't go near foreign exchange myself. Still, good luck.'

'Thanks,' I said, and walked upstairs to the spring sunshine.

The City seemed to have lost some of its charm over recent weeks. Even Townsville was attractive by comparison. I walked down Poultry and around the Bank. A bloke in a pink jacket and top hat looked at me suspiciously. If the Bank had had windows, I would have put a boot through one, I don't mind telling you. Maybe that's why it hadn't got windows. The guv'nor knew the anger of a dispossessed peasantry. I walked on. The City is full of history. The trouble is you don't notice when you're making money. It's only when the chips are down that the history in the shape of a bloke in a pink jacket and top hat comes out of the woodwork to mock you.

I wondered how long it would take to climb the Monument and throw myself from the top. But they must have known that people who had lost money might try to commit suicide so they had put wire netting over the balcony. Anyway, I'd probably be worn out before I reached the top. And what's the point of ending it all, Sid, old son, I asked? The Bundesbank – I wonder if Villi knew anything about that? – might still come in with support and you could make a fortune. On the other hand, the

Japanese might seize the opportunity to repeat Pearl Harbour and then you'd really be up the creek.

At last, I could stand the tension no more and went to the bank to see Barry. He saw me standing there and tried to avoid my eyes. New York was pretty hectic, said the bird who showed me in, and would I mind waiting until the panic was over?

'Can I get you a cup of coffee?' she asked.

'No, thanks,' I said. 'It might trigger off a heart attack.'

'I can make decaffeinated, if you'd prefer?'

In about ten minutes, Barry swivelled round in his seat and came towards me. I could tell by his expression that the news was not good.

'The news is not good,' he said. 'The dollar's taken a hell of a bashing. The European central banks all seem to have washed their hands of it.'

'What does that mean as far as my one-month dollars in Tokyo are concerned?'

'It means that, thanks to the failure of European bankers to put their money where their mouths are . . . '

'How much have I lost?' I demanded.

'All of it,' said Barry. 'And I'm afraid you owe us about twenty grand on top.'

'Only twenty grand?' I asked, suppressing an urge to giggle. 'Not fifty thousand or a hundred thousand?'

'I'll let you know the exact amount when we've worked it out,' said Barry. 'I'm sorry, Sid, but you know I did my best.'

Laughter, they say, is good for you, especially during moments of stress and financial haemorrhage. I began to chuckle, softly at first, then with fewer inhibitions. Finally, I abandoned all pretence at self-control.

The bird near the teleprinter cast an anxious glance in my direction. So did the dealers. Barry was getting perturbed. It was off-putting having a client with hysteria when everybody was trying to concentrate on the dollar-drachma cross rate. Besides, it was the second time I had thrown a fit in this particular bank. One more, and they'd probably refuse to deal for me, anyway.

'Would you like to come into the manager's office?' asked

Barry, ushering me towards the door. 'We've got a little something to perk you up there.'

'No, thanks,' I said, holding my stomach. 'I'm just a little punch drunk, that's all.'

'We're all a bit like that today,' said Barry. 'There have been some terrible losses.'

'So long as I haven't borne the brunt of the U.S. deficit all on my own,' I said.

'Oh, Christ, no! You'd need a lot more than a hundred grand to do that.'

I stumbled towards the door and tried not to think of the Monument. Or the river.

'Let me know how much I owe you,' I said, 'and I'll put a cheque in the post.'

15. Tomb with a view

The Hospital for Nervous Diseases, which I had always taken to be simply part of the landscape, a few NHS buildings not yet flogged off to property developers, suddenly assumed a more sinister appearance. Who were the patients, I wondered. Were they simple souls whose mental mechanism had somehow gone astray? Or were they perfectly normal people who had invested in stocks and shares and in the process lost touch with reality? Whoever they were, they had my sympathy. There but for the grace of God goes Sid, I thought.

I was on my way to see Mrs S. and her intended on the night before their nuptials. By rights, of course, they shouldn't have seen each other the night before but when the groom sort of lives there already there's not much point in sticking to tradition. I had got them a small wedding present, not much because the old bank balance was almost back to its pre-pools level. But when your broker and your former landlady are getting hitched you've got to push the boat out, at least far enough for it to float.

As usual, Freddy opened the door.

'Sid, my dear chap! This is a pleasant surprise. And just in time to prevent a pre-nuptial canter.'

Mrs S. was prancing about like an excited schoolgirl. I suppose she had been a schoolgirl once, a long time ago. But she was a fine-looking woman, all right, I could see what old Freddy had seen in her. Not everything, of course, because . . . well, I expect Freddy had seen things that I hadn't seen. But I could see enough to know that the old boy had made a wise choice.

'A little something to wet the brides's head?' he enquired, poised over a whisky bottle that I had not seen displayed in such a prominent position before.

'Just a little one, then,' I said. 'As a matter of fact, I've come to discuss a rather delicate subject.'

'Nothing is too delicate to discuss between friends,' said Freddy, pouring a generous tot. 'Fire away.'

'The fact is,' I began, hoping not to cast a shadow over their wedding, 'that since I have begun to invest in our enterprise society . . . '

'Out with it, old chap. What's the problem?'

'The problem is that I have lost all the money I won on the pools – or most of it, anyway.'

'Good God!' cried Freddy, aghast. 'I know we made a bit of bloomer on those African things but what about ICI? I thought you had a stack of those?'

'All gone,' I said. 'And the B.P., and the Marks and Sparks. How and where, I don't know, except that I have helped to subsidise the U.S. trade deficit. And so,' I added, glancing at Mrs S. who had remained very quiet throughout my tale of woe, 'I have come to collect what's left from under the mattress.'

Mrs S. blanched a little and averted her eyes. Freddy tugged gently at his moustache.

'I thought that if you just popped it in a plastic bag I could take it with me and I wouldn't have to disturb you on your honeymoon.'

The room seemed strangely quiet all of a sudden. I could hear the grandfather clock ticking quite plainly in the hall.

'Bit awkward at the moment, old chap,' said Freddy at last. 'You see, we put it in the bank . . . for safety, of course. I know that Isobel wasn't supposed to tell anybody but living in the same house you sort of find these things out, especially as it was under the mattress.'

'Oh, that's all right, then. Which bank did you put it in?'

Freddy swallowed. Mrs S. looked as if she was going to burst into tears, which she did.

'Oh, Sid!' she cried. 'How can we ever explain? You won't believe it, I know.'

'Believe what?' I asked, disturbed by this new turn of events. I had never seen Mrs S. so upset before. The opal brooch on her bosom quivered fit to bust.

'Oh, Sid! And you to be our best man, too!'

Mrs S. sniffed and wiped her nose on a delicate white tissue plucked from a box on the table. The spectre of the Hospital for Nervous Diseases once again loomed large.

'The fact is,' said Freddy, pulling himself together and finding his voice, 'that when I said it was in the bank that was not quite an accurate description of its whereabouts.'

'Where is it, then?'

'It has been put to very good use and you will have it just as soon as I can arrange a mortgage,' Freddy promised. 'In the meantime, it's as safe as houses. In fact, it is a house, or at least, part of one.'

'You didn't . . . ?'

Words failed me. Surely, not another victim of the Medway Building Society?'

'Oh, Sid!' wailed Mrs S., giving full rein to her emotions, 'we only did it because I wanted to be near Mother.'

'I thought Mother was dead?' I said, rather harshly.

That only made Mrs S. wail even more. Freddy appeared mightily embarrassed by this public display of slipped lippage.

'Now, now, my dear,' he said soothingly. 'We won't get anywhere if you make an exhibition of yourself.'

'It was your idea!' screeched Mrs S., pointing an accusing finger at her husband-to-be. 'You said we should take the money and put it to some use. Sid knows I wouldn't have touched it unless I had been forced to, don't you Sid?'

'Of course,' I said. 'But somebody please tell me: where is the money if it's not in the bank?'

Freddy seemed very contrite.

'I must admit that it was entirely my idea,' he confessed. 'Isobel is not in any way to be blamed.'

'Yes, but where is it?' I persisted.

'We used it to put a deposit on a house.'

'On a horse?'

'On a house . . . house,' said Freddy, repeating the word for my benefit. 'In the cemetery. You see, when they failed to find oil, the builders had the option to acquire the land.'

'Yes, yes. Renaissance Homes, I know all about them.'

'Well, Isobel and I were thinking about where we would live after our marriage and I rather liked the look of the houses they were putting up there.'

'And it was right on top of where Mother had been,' chipped

in Mrs S., sniffling badly. 'So how could we not buy?'

I understood. Even a millionaire minus his millions could grasp the need for security felt by his fellow mortals.

'But the houses are not built yet,' I said.

'No,' Freddy confirmed. 'But the demand for them is so great that we had to get in while they were still available. I mean, it's not every day that you have the chance to own a plot in a privatised graveyard.'

'But what about this place? You could have raised the deposit by selling this.'

'The landlord might have objected,' said Freddy.

'But . . .'

'You thought I owned it,' said Mrs S., smiling through her tears. 'No, I pay rent, like everybody else. Not everybody is an owner-occupier, you know.'

'I do know,' I said, bitterly.

I took a slug of whisky. Now, here's a how d'you do, I thought. A pretty kettle of fish. If they had used my money as a deposit, I should be entitled to a mortgage over the property, at the very least. They hadn't stolen the money because they had admitted taking it. Bit like joy-riding. Yobboes didn't steal cars any more; they just took them for a burn. I wondered how Stubbs would view the situation. He would no doubt take a strictly legal view and insist that justice takes its course. But how could I, Sid Arbuthnot, lay a charge against Mrs S. and her fellow joy-rider? Of course I couldn't.

'As soon as the house is up and running, I'll be able to arrange a mortgage – non status – and you can have your money back,' said Freddy. 'It's just that no building society, or even insurance company, will lend on what at the moment is no more than a gleam in a developer's eye.'

'And where is the money now?' I asked, conscious of having put that question once before.

'It's with Renaissance. They're holding it, subject to their receiving a better offer.'

'And what if Renaissance goes bust?'

'No chance of that, old chap. Not sitting on a chunk of prime real estate that has been virtually expropriated from the ratepayers.'

'I suppose not,' I conceded.

'The only unknown factor,' said Freddy, 'is time. How long it will take to get through the planning process and then round up enough Irish labourers to dig the foundations is anyone's guess.'

'Suppose it goes to appeal? That can take years, sometimes.'

'Well, yes, that's something I hadn't considered,' admitted Freddy.

'Oh, Sid!' wailed Mrs S., on the verge of tears again, 'you won't snatch the roof from over our heads, will you?'

Well, this just shows how much the situation has changed, I thought. Six months ago, Mrs S. could have chucked me out on the street to fend for myself or perhaps put up at Frank's place for a night or two. But she didn't. She let me stay there, not unmindful of the rent that hadn't been paid but not saying anything to exacerbate the situation. At least, not more than once a week. How could I chuck her out now, and on the eve of her wedding, too?

'Of course not,' I said. 'But as soon as you get back from your honeymoon I'll have my solicitor draw up a mortgage.'

'That's extremely decent of you, old boy,' said Freddy. 'I always knew we could rely on you. By the way,' he added, 'I've had a word with my friends about the placing. They say that as a special favour to me they might be able to help.'

'How much will that involve?' I asked, having to think about the pennies for once.

'The more the merrier, of course,' said Freddy. 'I've asked them to put you down for fifty thou. but whether you'll get them or not is another matter.'

'I don't know if I can afford fifty thousand, anyway,' I said, 'what with the U.S. trade deficit and all that.'

'But you must, old boy,' Freddy insisted. 'You can't turn down a placing that's pitched 15 per cent below market value. Guaranteed to make money.'

'Well, we'll see how many they come up with,' I said.

'Good show!' cried Freddy. 'We'll soon have you back on the road to financial health.'

I did not go to the wedding. By the time I had got home and checked my assets I was in no condition to go anywhere. The pain which had appeared in my right ventricle over the past few days was there again in the morning and throbbing away like nobody's business. I wondered whether to go to the doc. or whether, as it was Saturday morning and there was a big 'Save our NHS' demo in Trafalgar Square that afternoon, he would insist that I seek private attention. I phoned Mrs S. and made my apologies. She was very understanding. In fact, she thought it best in the circumstances that I stayed where I was and did not exert myself.

'I'll get the rabbi to give me away,' she said.

Freddy was as good as his word, though. On Tuesday morning, I received a letter from this firm of blue-blooded brokers offering me a few shares in a little company that was making a bomb by providing computer services for companies that were too small to invest in a computer themselves. I thought that almost anyone could afford a computer these days but perhaps I was wrong. Anyway, the brokers said that Greengage was doing all right and that they were doing me a favour by letting me have a share of the action. Well, you can't go wrong when dealing with the cream of the City so I dashed off a cheque and sent it away with the application form. If Freddy reckoned they were being offered at a 15 per cent discount, that was an easy ten grand just for the asking. Of course, it was peanuts compared with the amount I had lost but at least it was a step in the right direction. What's more, I was in with the right crowd now and in the City it's not what you know but who you know. If wealth depended on what you knew, half the blokes I'd met would be out on their necks.

The immediate problem was finding somewhere to live. The hotel was comfortable enough but expensive when you stopped to add everything up. Besides, I hadn't got over the way they looked at me when the fraud squad arrived to discuss Siggy's disappearance. It's not what you know but who you know, even in the country.

I couldn't go back to Fulham, nor could I impose myself on Mrs S. when and if her new house took shape in the cemetery.

And to be quite honest I was glad to get out of London. The country was a lot cleaner and much cheaper, though not necessarily the south-east which had begun to look a bit pricey unless you had a million quid in the bank, which I hadn't. But with the ten grand I stood to make on the Greengage placing and the – do you know, I had never asked Mrs S. how much exactly was under the mattress? – well, however much it was, and it must have been a fair amount to satisfy the builders, I could put down a deposit on a nice little semi somewhere up on the Yorkshire moors, Thirsk, maybe. Or what about Wales? Property was pretty cheap there, provided you didn't tell the locals you had half a dozen other houses over the border, in which case they'd visit you with a burning torch during the eisteddfod. At a pinch, there was Northern Ireland, although I've never been very religious myself, personally. On the whole, I favoured Yorkshire and asked the newsagent to get hold of a couple of newspapers from that part of the world.

Stubbs, the solicitor, was extremely sorry to hear of my plans.

'You won't like it up there,' he said. 'They're different from us down here. Speak differently, think differently, act differently. Completely different world. You could almost say it's a case of them and us.'

'I know they eat differently,' I said. 'But I don't mind a bag of chips occasionally, myself.'

'Quite so,' said Stubbs. 'But not for breakfast every day.'

I knew he was exaggerating, possibly because he was in danger of losing a client to some firm in Leeds or thereabouts. I asked him how much I owed for the work he had done on my behalf.

'Well, in all honesty, old boy,' he said, 'I don't think I can charge you anything. After all, I suppose that if I had not suggested' – he emphasised the word suggested – 'that you put all your money into the Medway you might have had some left.'

'That's true,' I agreed.

'So, if it's all right with you, we'll forget about it. Put it down to experience.'

Quite a decent old stick, really, Stubbs, I suppose. A lot of lawyers would have shoved in a huge great bill and even charged mileage for taking me to view the debris.

The following morning I received a letter from a certain senor at the Bank of La Paz. It did not make pleasant reading.

Dear Mr Arbuthnot (it began),

We are at present holding a cheque for £102,000 drawn on your account in favour of Kleencove Securities Ltd.

As your current account has a credit balance of only £6,482.68, which is well below the level at which it would attract anything but a notional rate of interest, we are unable to pay the aforementioned amount unless we receive adequate funds.

We await your instructions.

Bastards! Just like a banker to worry about something as trivial as insufficient funds when a profit of ten grand is at stake. They might almost have been one of those banks that had caused me so much trouble and strife before the pools company had put them in their places. And to think that it wasn't even a British bank, but a foreign one, talking like that to an Englishman in his own country.

I got on the blower to the manager immediately.

'Listen,' I said. 'I've got to have the money to buy some shares. It's for a placing, guaranteed to make money.'

'If the bank lent on every dead cert, we'd have been insolvent long ago, Mr Arbuthnot,' he said.

'But you can hold the shares as security.'

I could hear him thinking.

'It's a possibility,' he said. 'But, of course, you have no guarantee that the market will hold.'

'But they're being offered at a fifteen per cent discount,' I said. 'The market won't fall that far.'

'You have no idea, Mr Arbuthnot, how many times I have been told that shares cannot fall in value, only to watch them collapse like a pack of cards.'

'But you must help me!' I pleaded. 'It's my last chance to salvage something from the wreckage.'

'Let me have a word with my colleague in securities,' the

manager said. 'I'll call you back shortly.'

The second hand moves very slowly when you're waiting for a financial decision that can make or break you. Eventually the telephone rang.

'Mr Arbuthnot,' the manager said. 'I've had a word with our securities analyst and quite frankly we don't think that this issue is likely to be successful. Computer services are a drug on the market at present and we expect a rash of insolvencies over the next year or two. In the circumstances, I'm afraid that we cannot help.'

'Does that mean you won't honour the cheque?'

'It does – unless, of course, you can forward sufficient funds by the end of the day.'

'Thanks very much, old chap,' I said. 'In the circumstances, I would very much like to close my account. And I won't wait till the end of the day. I'll do it now.'

I hung up. Bloody foreigners! You'd think they controlled the banking system instead of just having a branch or two here and there. I kicked the bed. It was stronger than I thought and I hurt my toe.

What to do now, then, Sid, old son? Get on to Kleencove and Co. and tell 'em there's been a dreadful mistake and I didn't want to share in their ill-gotten gains, anyway? Or just sit tight and hope that the nice South American gentleman would have second thoughts and pay the cheque after all. I mean, what could he do except bounce it? And it wouldn't exactly be the first time some jumped-up bank manager had done that to me. I decided to sit tight.

It can be pretty nerve racking just sitting tight and waiting for the postman to tell you whether the numbers have fallen into the right position or whether you will be hauled into court for issuing a cheque without sufficient funds, etc. I wondered, even at this late stage, whether I could work the old dodge that Frank and I had used in the beginning. I mean, if Senor Gonzales saw a hundred thou. being paid in, he might just give the okay and let me pay for the shares. Once I had got them, of course, it would be too late for the gentlemen of La Paz. I could slip out of the country for a few days while the bankers were at each other's throats. But no, maybe it wasn't such a good idea. Since becoming a shareholder, I had learned to act more responsibly where money was concerned. I decided to accept my fate. I looked in the F.T. for my horoscope. For some reason – probably because it might upset the markets – they don't run the stars in the F.T.

The letter from Kleencove arrived in the second post. It was short and to the point.

Dear Sir, We return your application, together with your cheque. We had understood that you were in a position to pay. Clearly, we were mistaken.

So that's that, Sid, old chap. Six thousand quid between you and the poorhouse. I hope the issue flops and Greengage gets egg all over its bloody face. Why couldn't they offer shares to the public, instead of keeping everything tied up and gift-wrapped for their special customers? Anti-democratic and not in keeping with the new, wider risk-spreading culture. Wouldn't have happened in Australia, I thought. Out there, even the Abos get a fair crack of the whip.

I decided I wouldn't go to Yorkshire, despite the lure of a chippy franchise and dirt cheap houses. I would stay in London, the financial capital of the world and starting point for the Docklands Light Railway. Perhaps I could even yet carve out a career for myself in the City. After all, I had quite a lot of experience now.

A couple of days later, in my new lodgings near the old Battersea power station, I was glancing idly through the F.T. when a headline caught my eye. 'Greengage in Italian software coup', it said. I read on. 'Shares in Greengage Computer Services soared in London yesterday after the company announced it had bought a controlling interest in an Italian software outfit. The deal was made possible by the success of the recent placing and by the continuing strength of sterling. Analysts said the company was set to dominate the European software scene'.

I wondered whether to cut it out and send it to Senor Gonzales. But South Americans are a bit touchy about the economic success of others and I didn't fancy an early-morning call by the Bolivian heavy mob. Instead, I decided to send away for a pools coupon. Lightning, after all, can strike twice.

Post scrip

Dr Mohamed Chunda Singh, consultant psychiatrist, writes:

I have examined the patient, Mr Sidney Arbuthnot, both in the secure wing at Fulham and at my surgery in Southall, to which he was brought immediately following his breakdown. He is clearly suffering from acute depression and has a well-developed persecution complex, verging on paranoia. It is hard to say without access to the patient's bank account what has brought on this dementia but it would appear that he has recently undergone a series of financial setbacks. He is reluctant to discuss matters, even under hypnosis (given, of course, under the most stringent medical conditions). All he will say is that his misfortunes are due to 'a bunch of bankers'. Indeed, in his delirium, he repeats the words over and over again, albeit in a very slurred fashion.

It is my professional opinion that the patient will not respond to therapy until he has purged his soul of the devils that torment him. He must be prepared to renounce the values of a capitalist society and embrace those of a kinder, gentler culture. Only then will he regain his equilibrium. It is my further opinion that conventional shock therapy will not work. Indeed, there is a danger that an electrical charge passing through an abnormally thick skull will induce a permanent black-out. I am firmly of the opinion that treatment must begin with the diet.

Like many people brought up in ignorance of the relationship between mind and body, the patient has been eating too much red meat. While not in itself the primary cause of insanity, it can, in conjunction with an excess of alcohol, lead to a dangerous build-up of toxins that need to be flushed from the system. I therefore recommend, as a starting point, a simple diet based on, say, textured soyabeans and the juice of a freshly-squeezed orange. From time to time may be added a lightly-boiled egg. This will undoubtedly help to clear the gut. I also recommend a change of scenery. A brief sojourn in a sunnier clime would take the patient's mind off matters closer to home which may, perhaps, have unfortunate associations. The Channel Islands would be ideal or, if funds permit, somewhere further afield, such as Australia.

It may be that, once the blood has been cleansed, the patient will make a spontaneous recovery. He can then continue his journey towards nirvana, untroubled by the pressures of an increasingly-materialistic world. In the meantime, however, he is clearly unable to make rational decisions for himself. I would hesitate to have him certified but I do most strongly urge the appointment of an adviser with power of attorney, especially where financial matters are concerned. If a suitable person cannot be found amongst the patient's own circle of friends, I would be happy to recommend somebody.

Mohamed Chunda Singh, MD,
National Hospital for Nervous
Diseases, Fulham.